ALFRED LOISY

CAMBRIDGE
UNIVERSITY PRESS
LONDON: BENTLEY HOUSE
NEW YORK   TORONTO   BOMBAY
CALCUTTA   MADRAS: MACMILLAN

A Mon Maître Père
en souvenir de sa veille
à Ceffonds, 23-24 juillet 1934,
et témoignage d'affectueux
respect.

A. Loisy

ALFRED LOISY

His Religious Significance

BY

M. D. PETRE

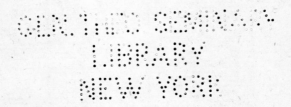

CAMBRIDGE
AT THE UNIVERSITY PRESS
1944

To
LOUIS CANET

PRINTED IN GREAT BRITAIN

CONTENTS

PART I

MAUDE PETRE

THIS study of the life and work of Alfred Loisy was the last of the many contributions of Maude Petre to the literature of the modernist movement in the Roman Catholic Church. It was completed shortly before her death in her eightieth year in December 1942. Several chapters were written during air raids, and others at intervals between fire-watching, attending a L.C.C. nursery where she was idolized by the children, and ministering to French and other refugees. Though the shades of the prison house grew deeper towards the end, the flame of her indomitable spirit burned more brightly. This volume therefore may be regarded as a memorial not only of the great French heresiarch who suffered the extreme penalties of the Church, but also of the author who once described herself as 'a solitary marooned passenger, the sole living representative of what has come to be regarded as the lost cause of modernism in the Catholic Church'.[1]

While it is true that a great soul has little need of ancestors Maude Petre showed in *My Way of Faith* (Dent) that she had a deep, inherited, but not uncritical, loyalty to her family tradition. She was the seventh child of a family of eleven, her father being the younger son of the thirteenth Lord Petre, a descendant of Sir William Petre, Under-Secretary of State in the reigns of Henry VIII, Edward VI, and Mary. Her mother, a daughter of the Earl of Wicklow, was a convert to Roman Catholicism. While maintaining unswerving loyalty to the Church, several of her ancestors also maintained a tacit, and sometimes an overt, resistance to the extreme claims of ultra-montanism. Thus despite the frequent fulminations of the Church against Freemasonry, which as early as 1738 had been banned by the Papal Bull of Clement XII, the ninth Lord

---

[1] *Vide* my article in *The Hibbert Journal*, July 1943, of which this introduction is an abridgement.

Petre, ignoring the possibility of excommunication, became the Grand Master of the English fraternity in 1772.

The characteristic thus exemplified was most deeply rooted in Maude Petre. Her almost 'ferocious independence', as she laughingly described it, above all in her spiritual relations, was, next to her abounding charity, the most fundamental trait in her rich and rare character. Where the soul was at stake she was as uncompromising as the most fanatical ultramontane who might wish to dictate to her. One of her earliest works, *Catholicism and Independence* (Longmans), was a call for spiritual liberty, for 'a faith not presumptuous but courageous even to audacity. To trust oneself is, in certain cases, to trust God, for if the light within be not from Him, then we are indeed of all men most miserable.'

The miracle was that she was able to maintain this rare independence of spirit with unwavering adhesion to the Church which had condemned her friends—Father Tyrrell whom it would have buried without a sign, Abbé Henri Brémond who was forced to retract his burial tribute in most humiliating terms, Baron Friedrich von Hügel who, although he escaped the major penalties, lived for many years under a cloud of suspicion from which he suffered deeply, and Loisy who gravitated after excommunication into complete severance from the Church, giving up all hope of a reconciliation, and even ceasing to desire it. To each of these leaders she was to the end, as Von Hügel used to address her, 'My brave dear Maude Petre'. She enjoyed their absolute confidence; they opened their hearts to her as to none other. She shared their troubles, and her courage and devotion provided a shield for them in the dark hours of their Gethsemane.

When she was required to give interior assent to a solemn condemnation of the cause of her friends as denounced in the Encyclical Pascendi of Pius X, without any assurance of its infallibility, but with the knowledge that it was the work of a reactionary ultramontane clique at the Vatican, and when she learned further that owing to the strong protest of the German Government at the time, many Catholics in the Reich were dispensed from the obligation to take the anti-modernist oath, her conscience and independence were outraged. She refused to take the oath, and, though often pressed to do so in later years, never wavered in her refusal. She would not compromise herself in this matter to the extent of von Hügel, who wrote to her in 1918:

It is forcibly in my mind—as far as I know myself—from a strong desire not to appear (it would be contrary to the facts and contrary to my ideals and convictions) as though all that action of the Church authorities had, in no way or degree, been interiorly accepted by me. Certainly that action was very largely violent and unjust; equally certainly, if one had been required definitely to subscribe to this or that document without express reservations, one could not, with any respect left, have done so.

For her refusal she paid the penalty of 'a partial local pseudo-excommunication', being forbidden to receive communion in the Southwark diocese, and deprived of graveside rites at her burial.

* * * *

In pursuance of her religious vocation she made a pilgrimage to Rome at the age of twenty-two on the advice of her Jesuit confessor, who prescribed a course of study in the philosophy of St Thomas Aquinas, as an elixir that would fortify her faith and dispel all doubt. This event caused as much surprise to eminent ecclesiastics as to her family at home. Her aunt, Lady Lindsay, explained to enquiring friends, that 'Maude had gone to Rome to study for the priesthood'. The Jesuit to whom she presented her credentials and explained her purpose could scarcely conceal his astonishment: 'You are the only one', he said dryly. Tyrrell, recalling the event many years afterwards, penned a valentine in which he depicted the passengers of 'The Rome Express' trying to push the train which had stuck on the line:

> Lo, in the rear an Amazon who shoves,
> And murmurs to herself: 'I feel it moves';
> Herself immobile, nothing can defeat her;
> Rock versus Rock, and Petre versus Peter.

On her return home she entered the sisterhood of 'The Daughters of Mary', a community founded in France during the Revolution, having houses in many parts of the world, and there she displayed such zeal in promoting orphanages, settlements amongst the poor, and in the instruction of converts, that she was eventually, as she said, 'kicked upstairs'. She was raised to the rank of Superior of the English and Irish Province, a position which she held with distinction for more than ten years.

About 1900, when she was thirty-eight years of age, she became closely acquainted with Father Tyrrell following a Retreat which he gave to the Sisters, and this acquaintance ripened into a long and noble friendship, until affection for him became the dominant interest of her life. To help him in his difficulties, to share his hopes and fears, to strive above all to maintain him in the Church, became an integral part of her vocation. His debt to her abiding affection especially during the last tragic phase of his storm-tossed career, when she proved herself hard as a diamond and more tender than a mother, when but for her devoted ministration he would have died outcast and unhouselled, was incomputable in mortal eyes. To those who implied a reproach for what they regarded as reckless unorthodoxy in befriending a heretic she replied: 'I could never do less for man in order to think more of God.' The tragic story which she told in her *Life of George Tyrrell* (Arnold) silenced the ecclesiastical watch-dogs: whether from fear or shame they thrust the book on the Index, praying no doubt that it would be remembered against them no more for ever.

Some years earlier she relinquished her position as Mother Provincial of the Sisterhood in a deeply affecting farewell. She could not reconcile her life-long faith as a loyal daughter of the Church with the harsh military conception of obedience and authority enforced by the Vatican in the name of Pius X. This was for her then and always the root problem of the modernist controversy.

'My first resolution to take a definite line', she wrote to a friendly priest, 'even in external matters in regard to Church authority dated from the condemnation of Abbé Loisy and not from any event in Father Tyrrell's career.'

That condemnation had made it clear to her conscience that the time had come for any who felt they had something to say to say it regardless of consequences. But as she explained to the next in authority in the Sisterhood: 'Of this you may be assured—even if I have to pain friends I will do my best never to be pained by them, because I will try to see motives of conscience and not of unkindness in anything they may do.'

She remained in this disposition to the end. No ostracism or deprivation could embitter her, no suffering cause her to lose faith and hope. When the cause seemed lost irretrievably and her friends were thrust 'like foolish prophets forth', she never ceased to work and pray that the Church might yet be freed from the dead hand of the past that it might enter into new life and holiness. She never lost the vision of that ampler day when the stone which the builders had rejected would become the corner-stone of the Temple, and the Church of the future would learn to revere the memory of those modernist martyrs who had lived and died His ambassadors in bonds.

JAMES A. WALKER

CARDIFF
December 1943

PART I

CHAPTER I

INTRODUCTION

THIS WORK is, in the first place, a war work, by which I do not mean that it represents any form of direct war service, but that it is being written under war pressure, and can be termed a war work as children born during this period are called war children.

Secondly, it is a work of friendship, for with its subject I enjoyed years of intellectual and sympathetic intercourse, which only ended with his death in 1940.

Thirdly, it is the work of a Catholic, a member of the Church from which Alfred Loisy was excluded, but of one who believes that, in spite of the vicissitudes of his religious life, he had a message of religious significance to deliver to mankind from which Christianity, and even Catholicism, can draw profit.

Lastly, it is the work of an English writer on a distinguished Frenchman, and for this reason it has, surely, a claim on English sympathy; we have a call to do for them what they cannot do for themselves.

But the subject of these pages died before the worst had happened; he was fortunate enough not to witness the subjugation and humiliation of his country. His name was such that, in other times, his death would have been a world event, in so far as the world of religious history and science is concerned; and it is because I feel that the day will come when, once more, such a personality will rouse interest and curiosity that I, one of his few contemporaries, desire to make some record for the future of what he was and what he did.

But while giving some appreciation of his life in general, I desire, above all, to study him from the religious point of view. For it was religion that occupied him from first to last. Why did he devote all his time and learning to religious documents unless this were so? After his breach with the Church he might have turned to other subjects of research; but the Gospels held him—the Scriptures, ancient and new—and while there was, to my mind, a period of severely scientific, and almost hostile, temper to the Church and even to Christian faith, there was ever an inextinguishable attraction to all that concerned the history and process and actual condition of Christianity.

I will not deny that he gave, to many of us, moments of anguish; I will not pretend to believe that he never manifested prejudice and even one-sidedness in his advocacy of certain positions; but I maintain, notwithstanding, that he was, even in spite of himself, irresistibly bound to the cause of religion, in some form or other.

And this is why I am anxious, in this study, to discover what, in the course of his long and tireless life, he did for or against the cause of religion, for or against the cause of the Christian religion in particular, for or against the Catholic Church, to which he first belonged and which later he repudiated. I am quite aware that the ordinary Catholic, who knows anything about his history, will exclaim that he did nothing for, and much against, the Church. He was condemned and he never submitted, and, for most, that is enough. That is enough in one sense. We cannot belong to the Catholic Church and not respect her decisions. But the Church has had a long history already, and has perhaps (surely so, in the belief of Catholics, if the world goes on) a long history yet to come; and even though she never repudiates her solemn actions, and will never say that Loisy was right and she was wrong, it may be that there are points in his teaching that will eventually prove to have an apologetic value even for her.

But, above all, his figure in future Church history is of the greatest importance, as no one more clearly than he has presented the problem of a spiritual body with an historic founda-

tion. Very few of those who criticized and condemned him
fully realized the magnitude of this problem, and its unavoidable influence on faith. Those for whom faith was a negligible
factor in the life of mankind had no reason to concern themselves
with what it might gain or suffer from its contact with history.
Those for whom history could be suppressed or set aside in
the interests of faith had no reason to trouble about what
historians might think or say; if their discoveries ran contrary
to the dictates of faith, those discoveries were false and their
advocates should be silenced.

But the problem remained; and whereas a man like Loisy
might easily, and perhaps did for a time, adhere to the former
class, he could never finally belong to it. For the Christian
faith remained a fact, and a fact of world significance, and its
historical character was, in a sense, unique in the general
history of religions.

I well remember a remark he made at a meeting at Pontigny,
when, speaking of religious origins in general, and of the fact
that the majority claimed their origin from some mythical personality, he pointed out that the Christian religion was unique in
its possession of a true historical personage as its founder. And
we shall see later how little patience he had with all attempts at
leaving Christianity standing without the historic Christ.

In studying the successive phases of his life and thought we
shall see how his conception of Christianity, as a vital factor
of human life, persisted through every stage of his evolution;
and how that conception seemed to grow stronger as his mind
was progressively freed from the actual bitterness that resulted
from the period of ecclesiastical conflict.

To anyone undertaking such a study as lies in front of me,
a particular method of treatment will suggest itself. I am not
attempting a biography of Loisy; his own autobiography is
ample in facts and matter.[1] What I shall try to do is to present
the leading characteristics of his work and teaching from the
religious point of view. And if some should object that this
is to take a one-sided view of my subject; that Loisy is interesting

[1] *Mémoires*, etc.

for the scientific and not the religious quality of his work, I still hold my own, and maintain that the main interest of his life was a religious one; and that his purely exegetical work falls into the category of other exegetical work, to which it is additional, of which it may be corrective, in which it may be permanent or merely evolutionary in character. (For he was ever himself conscious that exegesis was a science, like all sciences, ever in movement, never at rest.) But the bearing of science on religion was, at bottom, what really mattered in his eyes; and this is why I believe that he may eventually figure as one that upheld religious values in a time of crisis, and worked for the religious evolution of mankind.

It is my opinion, and I only put it forth as such, that he passed through phases in which personal suffering obscured the clearness of his vision. I think also that he was, from time to time, dominated by the attraction of certain theories of human philosophy. But through all ran an unbroken thread of religious faith and belief, and the Loisy who died in 1940 was nearer to the Loisy of early priesthood than to the storm-tossed Loisy of the Modernist period.

I remember a remark he made to me in response to a letter he had received from von Hügel regarding one of his more directly religious *opuscula*. The Baron had not shown himself sympathetic to these works, and seems to have suggested to him that his proper field of work was that of criticism.

'I could do that form of work by the hour', he said to me; 'these other works are my own'.

And so this study will be concerned with the religious aspect of his teaching only; this is its sole interest. I am in no way competent to appraise the value of his strictly scientific work, which will find its place in the process of historical studies in general; but from the moment of his death I felt, as never before, that there was a true religious value to be extracted from his shorter works, which were, as he said, *his own*— coming, as they did, from heart as well as head. This has been my sole aim, and the first part of my book is simply a preparation for the second part.

CHAPTER II

FAITH & ORTHODOXY

ALFRED LOISY was born February 28th, 1857, at Ambrières (Marne), of a family of what he termed 'agricultural workers'; I think the French term 'cultivateurs' would describe the position, and I fancy they would correspond to our English yeomen. His parents cultivated their own land, as their forbears had done, from father to son, for generations. His natural destiny would have been to follow the family career, and it was only the accident of weak health that altered the course of his life and turned him eventually to the priesthood.

I cannot but think that the generations of assiduous labour, though of a very different order, which preceded him, were responsible for something in the habits of indefatigable work in which his life was passed. And, like the peasant, he was a daytime worker; early riser and early to rest. Another inherited characteristic was his love of the land; of his garden and his livestock, to which he devoted his spare hours during the years when he lived in the country. And yet another family characteristic was his love of home. 'The life of a boarder', he says of his first school, 'was particularly disagreeable to me.' He drifted homewards on every possible occasion for legitimate rest, and it is a curious fact that the criticism of his fellow-clergy, directed against this love of home, exercised an influence on his future when it became the indirect cause of his first relations with Duchesne, and his more exclusive dedication to the life of study.

He recounts the incident in the first volume of his *Mémoires*. He had been appointed to the parish of Landricourt, which was in reach of Ambrières, where his family lived. It was a little village of about 125 inhabitants—with its unfailing (in that land) touch of anti-clericalism; but where the *curé* was respected and the church fairly well attended.

The presbytery...was only two and a half kilometres from my home. There was nothing easier than to make frequent visits to my parents, without any failure of duty, nor any unfavourable criticism....I lived there very quietly, preparing my sermons and catechisms, and fulfilling the ritual which my predecessor had elaborated. All this left me plenty of free time for my modest studies, and I should have been quite content if a neighbouring *curé* had not complained to the bishop that my family was a prejudice to my ministry.

There followed an insinuation in an address by Mgr Meignan, his bishop, in which he hinted that

there used not to be difficulties in the parish of Landricourt. All the *curés* looked at me and I at them, and I began to think that it might be wiser to provide for my own future, unless I was to be passed from parish to parish until the end of my days.

He confided his troubles to a friend who was living with Duchesne; the latter had well estimated the intellectual qualities of the young priest, and was eager to draw him into the work for which he believed him to be exceptionally fitted. And so the wanton criticism of a confrère was partly the occasion of his exclusive dedication to the work of his life. Without that incident he might have combined the life of parish priest with that of a student and writer, and his life would have followed other lines.

But this happened in 1880, when he was already a priest, and we have now to follow him in the first steps of his profession, and the corresponding impressions.

The notion of the priesthood came to him suddenly on one occasion when he was hearing Mass at Ambrières, but his decision was made in October 1873, during the course of a retreat.

'Having no taste for any secular profession I determined to give myself to God'; which resolution he carried out in spite of the objections of his family. He entered the seminary of Châlons-sur-Marne, with ardour and piety, but, like many another, he found that perfection was not to be found even in an ecclesiastical seminary; that there were sharp lines of division between opposed schools of thought; and that, above all, the demands of orthodoxy were not always consistent with what he esteemed the demands of truth.

As regards the conflicting views that he found in the seminary, he says:

I had to learn that there existed different tendencies in French Catholicism. Only four years had passed since the famous Council, and there were still witnesses of the clearance which Mgr Meignan had effected in 1871, by the substitution of a body of more moderate men for the ferocious band of Ultramontanes. He had, however, only half succeeded.[1]

These two schools would not have been without their influence on the more vital question of the relations of faith to orthodoxy.

Pour vous toujours la vérité, jamais l'orthodoxie, was the advice of Abbé Huvelin to Friedrich von Hügel. But the latter was a layman, whereas the young ecclesiastical student was brought into more direct and material contact with the demands of the orthodox school.

And now I transcribe his own words, which were, of course, written long after the seminary crisis, and which express his later and mature opinion on the subject, not the opinions and feelings of the young seminarist, to whom the question was one of conscience, with the possibility of sin.

This question of orthodoxy, its rights or wrongs, is acquiring fresh interest and importance in the present day. A recent writer in the *Hibbert Journal* speaks deprecatingly of the 'aim, of younger men especially, to galvanize into an appearance of life' the 'dogmatism of the past'. We have the Barthian movement, with its roots in the philosophy of Kierkegaard— we have such an inspiring writer as D. R. Davies in his *On to Orthodoxy*. All this gives fresh significance to a study of the experience of Loisy in his seminary days. For it was dogmatism, as enshrined in orthodoxy, that came athwart his early and enthusiastic faith; it was indeed for him definitely a contest between his sense of truth and the claims of religious belief.

[1] *Mém.* I, 37.

There was then an intellectual movement, on the part of
Christian believers, against the dogmatic spirit; there is now an
intellectual movement, on the part of a school of Christian
believers, in its favour. Is it a case of downright contrariety
between the two schools; or can the later one have, in part,
sprung from the former? It seems to me that the question is
rational and legitimate.

Orthodoxy (writes Loisy in his *Mémoires*, when treating of
his seminary days) is, in a sense, the mother of heresy, and
we may add that the converse is also true. For orthodoxy is
a myth. There is no such thing as an unchanging doctrine.
A contradicted doctrine is dissipated...or transformed. The
orthodoxy of to-morrow will not be that of yesterday but a
cross between that orthodoxy and the heresy of to-day....From
the moment that a religion claims to teach an unvarying doctrine it goes against the law of nature and humanity...for
it is impossible for human thought to be immobilized in ideas
that are subject to the action of experience and reflection.[1]

But these are later reflections. Loisy arrived at the seminary
inspired by the traditional faith of his early upbringing. To
quote his own words:

During the first months of my life in the seminary I was
impressed above all by the exercises of piety, the well chanted
liturgy, the ceremonies of the Cathedral. I delighted in the
morning meditation, to which I devoted myself with simple
fervour; no least cloud of doubt yet troubled my relations with
the Divine world. The chants of the Church sometimes plunged
me into a kind of tender ecstasy. I remember particularly the
sentiment of divine melancholy with which the hymn of
Placare, Christe, servulis, of the vespers of All Saints, filled me.
But the more intense became my spiritual and mystical ideal
the more it seemed to me that the life of the secular clergy
did not wholly respond to it, and that to serve God perfectly
it would be necessary to enter a religious order.[2]

It was only the advice of his confessor that held him back from
the fulfilment of this latter design; and we may note again the
curious fact that, in this instance as in the later one already

[1] *Mém.* I, 35.   [2] *Idem,* I, 40–41.

quoted, it was from members of the clergy that came the check to the fulfilment of a life that might have run on very different lines from those which it eventually followed.

Those early criticisms are not uncommon in youth which is over-earnest; and, as he tells us, Loisy came later to a juster estimate of his fellow-students.

But, after this moral shock, there came a disturbance of his happy religious optimism arising, not from dogmatic intransigence, but from the divisions of opinion between his teachers in regard to the burning question of papal infallibility as recently defined.

For now another veil, that of the Temple itself, was rent, and I saw that there were differences even between the Princes of the Church. A solemn dogma had just been defined, though the majority of French bishops was opposed to its promulgation; was it thus that truth was to be established in the Roman Church? And that was not all. The most sympathetic personalities of contemporary Catholicism, an Ozanam, Catholic apologist and founder of the Conferences of St Vincent of Paul; a Lacordaire, eloquent ascetic, whose pulpit...had been an intellectual centre; a Montalembert, champion of religion and its rights, were all denounced as suspects by people who claimed the authority of the Pope and were not disowned by him. Even my master, confessor and friend, the Abbé Ludot... was classed with these suspects....

My inexperience and complete ignorance of the world and of history prevented me from understanding the true meaning of these disputes, which, nevertheless, disconcerted me.[1]

I do not know whether the present generation is capable of suffering as did that of Loisy—and my own—from the discovery of imperfection in what they had deemed perfect. The critical spirit awakes earlier in our day; or is it that there is less tendency to idealization? Anyhow we may take it that the perception of these differences, between men whom he had conceived as wholly united in truth and charity, was no light trial to the young and ardent seminarist. It was the first step to a conception of the graver problem that was next to face

[1] *Mém.* I, 44.

him, that of the apparent opposition of the orthodox and strictly dogmatic expression of religious truth to its mystical and spiritual meaning—and, later on, to the liberty of scientific thought.

And let it be noted that the struggle which we are to witness in the mind of our subject is only conceivable because he was earnestly religious. Amongst what we may describe as orthodox believers more than one type may be distinguished. To name two or three of these types, there is the reasoning and rationally convinced orthodox believer; there is the unreasoning, simple earnest believer, who has no doubts because he is wholly certain that what the Church says is true; there is the indifferent orthodox believer, who never troubles his head on the subject and takes the whole teaching of the Church in his stride, because his stride is in quite other directions. I have met with minds of this third category who are contemptuous of any criticism in religious questions, simply because they regard the official element of the Church as analogous to a business company, entitled to settle its own affairs without interference; quite overlooking the fact that every member of the Church has a life and death interest in her teaching and truth; whereas a business concern has a restricted commercial interest for those who take part in it. The employés of a financial company can live without it, can turn their attention elsewhere, the children of the Church do not think they can live without her; hence, in the case of thinking Catholics, the trouble of mind when orthodox pronouncements seem either to lessen the spiritual presentation of religious truth or to run counter to human knowledge. It is not so much what orthodox statements *contain* that troubles the mind of the religious questioner, as what they *exclude* or repress; when they repress the spontaneous spiritual movement of the soul, or when they exclude, or seem to exclude, plain scientific truths. If we turn to Loisy's history of his seminary days we shall see how these two points emerge from his personal experience.

From the time that he commenced his theological studies he tells us that his troubles began:

The presentation of Catholic belief, as set forth in the dogmatic and moral theology of the Church, began to fill both mind and conscience with invincible disquiet.[1]

I should like to call attention to the word *conscience* as well as mind in this statement. For conscience said, on the one side, 'I have to believe what I am told'; while conscience said, on the other side, 'My soul is dissatisfied'. He had no Huvelin near him, with his dictum, 'Toujours la vérité jamais l'orthodoxie'; he had no Chestertonian solution of dogma as an anchorage rather than a cabin; the very character of his intellect would have made him positive and literal in his apprehension of doctrine; and yet there was another element of his mind that sought a wider and more spiritual interpretation of truth.

I have said elsewhere how the study of the Summa of St Thomas...increased my trouble instead of appeasing it. It was not good-will that was lacking in my endeavour to find truth in the scholastic doctrines...for I approached the subject with entire confidence.... The angel of the schools disconcerted me by the boldness of his logical constructions, for which I found no solid foundation; nevertheless he interested me more than his modern interpreters...these latter simply repelled me.[2]

He mentions some of them by name; those writers of scholastic manuals whom von Hügel once termed 'rascals like Liberatore!'

He found in Hebrew studies a relief from this torture; a relief which eventually proved more complete than he then foresaw.

This crisis endured from 1875 to 1879, though, as he adds, it continued at intervals after his ordination, and never really ended till 1908. But the special character of those troubled years was

a perpetual anxiety, without any definite approach to the peace that might have been gained, on the side of theology, by the triumph of mystical faith, on the side of free research by the abandonment of theological belief.... All the time that I spent in the seminary I accepted, with whole-hearted respect, the teaching that was given me in the name of the Church....

[1] *Mém.* 1, 50. [2] *Idem*, pp. 50–51.

I tried my best at scholastic studies. I undertook the study of the Scriptures because it was presented to me as the highest of the sacred studies. . . . It was without the least pride that I suffered, asking myself if all that was true, and forbidding myself to think that it was not. I did not take the obligation to believe in the teaching of the Church at all lightly, I regarded unbelief as a grave sin and a misfortune. . . .

I will not flatter myself that I had any experience of the high states of contemplation; but I was not without experience of mystical fervour. . . . Mysticism had its adepts at the seminary of Châlons, and I was one of the most zealous. . . .

Until my ordination, and during the first years of priesthood, I cherished a fairly intense mystical life, though I was perpetually troubled by an anxiety the true nature of which was understood neither by myself, nor by the few to whom I revealed it. . . . M. Oury and M. Monier, to whom I gave a summary description of my state, and to whom I would have given further details had they asked for them, which they did not, treated my doubts as a kind of scruple or mental obsession, which it was better to ignore than to examine. They thought that the trouble would disappear, whether by the practice of the ministry and the regularity of my priestly life, or even by virtue of the serious studies I was undertaking. I thought I should accept their advice, as I had no sure motive for disputing their judgment, and as I desired nothing more than to recover my peace of mind in the possession of the faith which I still felt was mine and which I desired to preserve.

These prognostics might have been realized if I had not remained at the *Institut Catholique*, teaching subjects that impelled me to the fundamental examination of primitive documents and religious origins. They would have been realized if I had never come to Paris, and if the diocesan administration of Paris had been wise enough to employ me in some fairly active and interesting ministry, whose moral efficacity would have reassured me of the essential value of the cause I served. Many problems would have escaped my attention because I should not have had the time to discover them. I should not have developed much intellectually—a fate which befalls many, even intelligent, priests—and I should have grown old with the reputation of a good priest, a prudent director, and even a firm and diligent administrator. Fate had decided otherwise.[1]

[1] *Mém.* I, 59–64.

These last words recall to my mind a conversation I once held with Louis Canet, Loisy's devoted disciple, who knew him better than anyone knew him and who was also too independent minded to form anything but his own judgment even of his revered friend.

Referring to that incident in Loisy's later life, when an effort was made, on the part of some, to have him raised to a bishopric, I asked Canet what would have been the outcome of such a step. He answered me that he believed that Loisy would have become a great and noted bishop; implying that there would have been no retrogression, no 'gran rifiuto' of his true life, but another form of its fulfilment.

I should be sorry to think that my long quotation had only given the impression of the coming abandonment of faith. I see in it the expression of a problem that was with him to the end; the problem that besets many a religious mind when it becomes conscious, either of the chilling effects of rigid dogma on spiritual experience, or of the disturbing character of the conflict between orthodoxy and truth.

Into Loisy's account of those early troubles both these elements enter; his soul craved for a more spiritual apprehension of truth; his mind demanded a more scientific one.

In his spiritual reaction to theology there is a great likeness to the earliest, and most important, reaction of George Tyrrell to the same. In his article 'Theology and Devotion', which he regarded as the keynote of his whole teaching, he says:

I have more than once known all the joy and reality taken out of a life that fed on devotion to the Sacramental Presence by . . . a flash of theological illumination; and have seen Magdalens left weeping at empty tombs and crying: 'They have taken away my Lord, and I know not where they have laid Him.'

Beside this we may quote a note of Loisy's of July 11th, 1892:

What we have to do is to renew theology from top to bottom, to substitute the religious for the dogmatic spirit, to seek the soul of theological truth and leave reason free under the control of conscience.[1]

[1] *Mém.* I, 210.

But now we pass to the second point on which his mind came into conflict with orthodoxy. We have first the spiritual revolt, and next the intellectual one. It was the latter which finally separated him from that Church to which he had so ardently desired to adhere.

I take it that he little anticipated, when he first entered on his historical and exegetical studies, how far they would eventually lead him. He approached the Scriptures as one of the highest studies that could be undertaken; as the study of God's dealings with man. He found, first, that man had a greater part in those documents than that for which his early teaching had prepared him; he found, next, that these sacred documents, apart from the histories they related, had their own history, a history which he had never suspected. But he entered on his life-work in the full hope of remaining faithful to tradition while facing all the problems of history that he would have to encounter. He hoped, as he says in one place, to refute Renan by his own methods, and in his dedication of his *Histoire du Canon de l'Ancien Testament* to his pupils, 1890, he says:

Throughout this work I have endeavoured to reconcile sound criticism with tradition, to unite the prudence of the theologian with the sincerity of the scholar, not sacrificing either. If perchance I have not succeeded too badly I shall be more confident in expounding, presently, the history of the Canon of the New Testament.

He adds:

I do not think I ever renewed these declarations. It seems to me . . . that the last words present with some faithfulness the attitude that I wished to adopt, and that I tried to maintain, until ecclesiastical censure overtook my writings.[1]

During the scholastic year 1890–1891, his theme was, first the Canon of the New Testament, and next the Book of Job. Meanwhile M. Vigouroux was lecturing in the same Faculty, and in the Calendar it was announced that he would 'investi-

[1] *Mém.* I, 191.

gate what and how much the authors of the Sacred Books drew
from contemporary times and matters'.

Loisy's comment on this announcement is:

Apparently inoffensive, but actually absurd, this pronouncement contains, in a scholastic form, the postulate of orthodoxy.
According to the general sense, a book cannot exist without
relation to the time and *milieu* of its production. . . . My little
works implied and explained that the Biblical writings were
composed under the same historical and psychological conditions as all books written by man, and that they were only
truly intelligible to the extent that critical history could inte-
grate them in their original time and environment; scientific
exegesis deals with their real character, the metaphysic of
inspiration evades all analysis.[1]

(I should like to revert to this last phrase later.)

In 1889, having passed through the early phase of trouble
and hesitation, Loisy, in possession of a chair at the *Institut
Catholique*, was preparing what he regarded as his life-work.

I had conceived (he writes) a programme of very simple, but
vast and logical teaching, which would have filled my life had
I been left free to fulfil it. My fundamental thought, which
I did not utter too clearly, was that there was no scientific
study of the Bible in the Catholic Church, and that it had to
be created by shifting. . .questions of Biblical introduction
and exegesis from the theological and dogmatic spheres into
the sphere of history for rational and critical study. . . .
The starting-point was taken from the character of ecclesiastical belief in regard to the books that Christian tradition
regarded as sacred. The Bible is the collection of books that
the Church regards as divinely inspired.

The first question, then, would be:

How did the notion of divine inspiration arise, persist and
come to be defined, and how are we to understand it from the
point of view of historical and philosophical criticism?[2]

After enumerating the various points of his scheme, he continues:

This plan consisted in a vast scheme of research and a great
history to be constructed, the materials of which might have

[1] *Mém.* I, 193–194. [2] *Idem*, pp. 172–173.

been, in a great proportion, already elaborated by Catholic authors, but not comprehended in a single work of a strictly scientific character. I did not flatter myself that I could construct such a work in a day, nor even in several years, but I was prepared to consecrate my life to it; I thought I could thus employ myself usefully, being in possession of a critical method and equipped for exegetical work by my training as an orientalist. Furthermore, being convinced that theological orthodoxy could not in the long run prevail against scientific truth, but would be forced to reckon with it and accommodate itself to it, I did not think that the fact of having lost confidence in the absolute value of traditional dogmas unfitted me for the teaching of exegesis in a Catholic faculty. After all, was it not a service to the Church to invite and help her to free herself from a narrow and superannuated gnosis, which compromised her moral action on a world that was increasingly cultured?

Clever people, on the strength of what happened later, will not fail to say that orthodoxy is an impassable barrier, against which I could but speedily break myself. But such persons know, or ought to know, as well as I do, that orthodoxy is only unchangeable in the imagination of those who hold to it, and that this supposedly unchangeable doctrine has been continually modified in the course of centuries and that it is changed before our eyes, often, even by those who boast of protecting its inviolability. . . . Certainly the adoption or toleration of scientific methods by an institution like the Catholic Church is difficult, because great social institutions, particularly religious ones, are governed by routine, and because the Roman Church, in the interests of domination, claims to be unchangeable by principle and even by the Will of God; but it is not impossible, because this immutability is merely apparent and fictitious, because institutions only endure by adapting themselves to the changing conditions of humanity . . . because the Church herself has only lasted till now by thus adapting herself, consciously or unconsciously. The Church, composed of men and administered by men, is a human institution, and human institutions must be carried forward or destroyed in the vital evolution of human society.[1]

But this is not all that he had to say on the subject. Orthodoxy, for him, signified the intransigent defence of religious

[1] *Mém.* I, 175–176.

dogma, not in a purely spiritual, but in a quasi-scientific sense; for it seemed to him that theologians claimed for theology a double quality of certainty, the quality of faith and the quality of assured scientific truth. The dogmas of faith were true because the Church taught them as revealed truths; they were also true because history and science taught them as historical and scientific truths. It was the validity of this latter point that he denied.

Thus he says further on:

I had found a clear and advantageous distinction, in my principle of the truth of the Scriptures. There was the historical sense of the texts and their traditional one; the first appertaining to them in virtue of their origin and true nature, the second that which has been grafted on to them by the work of faith in the later evolution of Judaism and Christianity. For the critical historian only the first is to be considered as the meaning of the Biblical text; the second regards the history of exegesis and belief.

I think no critic would dare to deny the soundness of this distinction. On the other hand no one would complain because I did not shout out that traditional exegesis had been, in great measure, a tissue of contradictions. This is what it appears to us retrospectively, from the point of view of critical science, but from a human and philosophical point of view such contradiction is less worthy of note than the movement of thought, especially in ages when the historical spirit was little developed, and when the old texts served as a theme, or as a pretext for mystical speculation in harmony with fresh religious preoccupations, without any craving for a natural and primitive sense, of which there was no idea. . . .

The great—I might say the only—difficulty, against which I was to be broken, was real, substantial and living; it was the authority, or rather the tyranny, which in Roman Catholicism has supplanted, not only the Scriptures, but even tradition, and which aims at the domination of thought, history and politics. . . .

In taking possession of the Chair of Holy Scripture at the *Institut Catholique* of Paris I had no undue confidence in my youth and my limited science; but I was confident in the goodness of my cause, in the legitimacy of my enterprise, in the goodness of my action, notwithstanding the 'équivoque' which would inevitably result from the contact that had to be maintained with theology and the official teaching of the Church. Furthermore, I was certain that my hearers would be interested in my work, and I was determined to have regard for them and not to pass over the steps of the reform that appeared to me indispensable. I should have scrupled to trouble these young inexperienced minds, and I planned to furnish them, as I went on, with the solution of the difficulties that critical exegesis could not fail to arouse in its contact with traditional theology. A doubtful task perhaps; but I did not want it to fail through my fault. And I was encouraged by the confidence of the rector[1].[2]

And here I pause to ask myself whether it would, indeed, have been possible for Loisy to carry on the work he had planned; to carry it on as a Catholic, to carry it on as a priest. Would such a line of work and conduct, even had it not been roughly broken by the intransigence of the authorities with whom he came in contact, have been practical, without some subtlety and evasion? Would it have implied a kind of compartmental system of thought, theology in one division, history in another, while, unlike the division of sciences dealing with distinct subjects, both would have been handling the same theme from different standpoints?

This is the problem that, during all that period of growing exegetical awareness in Catholic minds, was consciously, almost agonizingly, studied by the faithful believer. A spiritual Church, with an historical foundation, presents a troublous proposition.

I do not say that Loisy had then a final and satisfactory answer to the problem. Had he continued on the same way, had he carried that *Livre Inédit* to its conclusion, he might have furnished a valuable solution. But even in what he contributed to the question there are thoughts worthy of consideration. He speaks of the 'tissue of contradictions' in Catholic exegesis, but he adds that such contradiction, 'from a human and philosophical point of view', is not so worthy of note as 'the movement of thought' which produced it in response to religious preoccupations, and in an age which had little regard for 'natural and primitive sense'.[3]

[1] Mgr d'Hulst.   [2] *Mém.* 1, 178–179.   [3] *Idem*, p. 178.

Elsewhere, as we have seen, he says that 'scientific exegesis deals with the real character of documents; the metaphysic of inspiration evades all analysis'.[1]

And when his bishop, Mgr Meignan, interrogated him as to his opinion on 'prophecies in general', his reply was: 'It seems to me, Monseigneur, that the prophetic books of the Old Testament are a collection of exhortations rather than predictions'; *prédications plutôt que prédictions*.[2].

In all this he is moving towards the position he maintained to the end—the literature of the Scriptures is the work of faith and not its cause and origin; Christianity has created its own literature, historical and scientific to a point, but only secondarily; the Church has preserved this literature, not as the proof of her teaching but as its outcome.

Perhaps, in her great unconscious manner, the Catholic Church herself may eventually absorb something of this apologetic as though it were her own; it is not for me to pass an opinion on the subject. But in studying this phase of Loisy's evolution I have been impressed by a certain analogy, remote indeed, but interesting, to a new school of thought in other Churches. There has been, in fact, an effort to constitute what I venture to term a kind of theological *by-pass*, for the passage of orthodoxy round the findings of history and science. I do not think that Loisy could have been quite at one with these later writers, nor they with him, but neither am I sure that his position may not have contributed to the fashioning of their thought. Is it possible that this new conception of what these religious thinkers term orthodoxy has been fostered by that early conflict in which Loisy both fought and suffered, and others with him?

Thus Mr D. R. Davies writes:

We are cradled in the idea that things must be either this or that. Either—Or! It requires an intellectual rebirth almost before we can realize that things can be both this and that.[3]

[1] *Mém.* 1, 194.   [2] *Idem*, p. 227.
[3] *On to Orthodoxy*, p. 64.

The evils of the pre-Christian world still abound in Christendom. That is not to disprove the faith of prophetic religion. On the contrary it is its profound and tragic corroboration. What it does disprove, of course, is the falsity of the Liberal denudation of Christianity, of its absolute, supernatural, non-historic essence.[1]

What started me on to the discovery of Orthodoxy, of New Testament, traditional Christianity? It was the desire and the need to work for social change, but with conviction, with hope and indeed certainty. I longed to recover whole-heartedness in the struggle for a different civilization.[2]

Now we have seen that it was the 'discovery of Orthodoxy' that first roused Loisy to a troubled examination of the faith with which he had entered on his first religious studies. Orthodoxy, as he was made to understand it, was not consistent with the freedom of historic truth—and, what mattered more, it did not seem to him consistent with the strictly spiritual character of Christianity. He saw a way through, though he had not as yet explored it; he saw a way that might be dark and dangerous; he had to choose between the dangers of that exploration and his anchorage in the Church; and we shall see that eventually he abandoned, not only his anchorage, but his efforts to justify the traditional teaching by a wider, a less dogmatic interpretation of its meaning. He had not begun as a free lance, as did the writer from whom we have quoted; he started from a defined position, and had to lose that position or keep it. But I think we can see, in those passages already quoted, a somewhat like attempt to reach a reality that was not dependent on its historic presentation, even though it manifested itself in historic garb.

Says the writer from whom I have quoted:

I am anxious to make it quite clear what I mean by orthodoxy. I do not mean by it the officially accepted creeds and confessions of the Church so much as the substantive experience and knowledge that are proclaimed in those Creeds. This involves, as I see it, a much deeper consideration of the Creeds themselves.[3]

[1] D. R. Davies, *On to Orthodoxy*, p. 94.
[2] *Idem*, pp. 112–113.   [3] *Idem*, footnote, p. 112.

Now this writer—and I suppose, still more, Karl Barth, to whose school (whether his scholar or not) he in some sense belongs—are men who have faced criticism in its fullest and most devastating force. They have not refused the lesson of history, but they have somehow looked *through* history, without denying it. Their faith is in a great spiritual reality, that might be presented, or misrepresented; stated or distorted; proved or disproved by history—that would never, in this life, be freed from its historic dependence, but that was, nevertheless, independent and self-sufficing.

There are some who must, like the rest of us, live by time, and yet for whom time falls away with the sense of eternity; and so, living in history, learning from history, some feel that the fact clothed in history has its own reality independent of history.

It is a new line of apologetic which I am not competent to judge. It has undoubtedly its way yet to go; but in reflecting on the first critico-religious experiences of Loisy, I ask myself if he was not preparing a conception of faith somewhat analogous to this later school. It was the theologico-scientific presentation of dogma that seemed to him an impoverishment of spiritual truth, a contradiction of historic truth. It was not dogmas, but their presentation, that troubled his early faith. But dogmas as divine utterances; truths with the solidity of stones, not arguable, not irrefutable, because they have no temporal attachment, no dependence on anything but their own force and substance; dogmas to be received by faith and not by reason; dogmas in such sense were partly adumbrated in his early efforts to reconcile human truth and divine revelation. As he said, in a passage already quoted, 'the metaphysic of inspiration evades all analysis'.

CHAPTER III

DUCHESNE

I REMEMBER well that, on the first appearance of Loisy's great autobiography, not a few, and I myself amongst them, were shocked at the severity of his judgment of many of his friends. Having been very gently treated myself, I have the less difficulty in according some justice to this view. Amongst those who seemed to suffer, rather roughly, at his hands was Duchesne. Now I have to admit that I had not long undertaken this work before I perceived that one's first view of his account of his relations with that great historian was not quite sound; that he states very fully all that he owed to Duchesne, all that Duchesne did for him, and all the much more that Duchesne would have done for him, but that he very soon realized that he must preserve his mental and spiritual independence, that there was a difference between them of aim and ideal, a difference of method, a difference of outlook, a difference of character.

Perhaps Loisy was not as grateful for Duchesne's very real goodness and affection as he ought to have been. Loisy had great powers of family affection, but I am not certain that he had such great power of friendship; I think his friends mostly felt that to disagree with him on any of his firm convictions would be to disagree with him altogether; and I know that one of his dearest friends never ventured to contradict him. He lived by mind rather than heart, and mental agreement was, for him, essential to friendship. We shall see how this affected another great friendship in his life. But with regard to Duchesne the differences were of a very vital character; he soon felt that he must follow or separate; and if Duchesne's friendship seems to have been of a wider and more tolerant kind this was, in fact, just because his power of tolerance, or, rather, indifference, was one factor of Loisy's distrust.

I should place the source of eventual disagreement under two main headings : first of all, a vein of cynicism, scepticism, levity, of which Loisy became quickly conscious in his friend; secondly, the resolute avoidance, on the part of Duchesne, of all Scriptural complications. Now had this been because Duchesne had no consciousness of the problems that would have to be faced on that subject, or because his faith in the Church's treatment of the Biblical question was untouched, then Loisy would have had no right to criticize or judge his conduct and attitude; but he knew, of course, the contrary, and even though Duchesne should not feel called on to devote himself to Scriptural exegesis it was not a subject which should, in Loisy's judgment, be evaded.

We are not bound to follow Loisy in all these views. By keeping his place in the Church, Duchesne did for her what he could not otherwise have done. By keeping his place in the Church, he also secured the peace of his own soul and his anchorage in the order of Melchizedek. My part, in this place, is only to show how a friendship, which might have exerted a permanent influence on Loisy's destiny, was first shaken, and eventually almost dissolved.

Loisy was in charge of a little parish, Landricourt, when, as we have seen, he first approached Duchesne, though not directly, for advice in regard to his studies. Duchesne had quickly realized the intellectual worth of this young priest, and was disposed to do all in his power to forward and facilitate his career. And for Duchesne it was a career which promised future honours. His friend must not vegetate in a country cure; Paris was his rightful place, and the Faculty of Theology in the *Institut Catholique* the right opening.

But Loisy had no wish to leave his cure and establish himself in Paris; and he had even avowed to his more ambitious protector, that he cared neither for university nor for theological degrees.

This annoyed Duchesne; it was a mark of eccentricity, and 'eccentric people are useless. . . . Make this sacrifice to the Church, which upholds such honours'.

'I do not think', Loisy remarks, 'that this eloquent and even edifying tirade had much effect on me. Later on, Duchesne will preach to me, with as much conviction and as little success, the excellence of academical honours and titles.'[1]

It was not, eventually, in deference to Duchesne, but in consequence of the trouble (already mentioned) that arose for him at Landricourt, that he took up what he hoped to be but a temporary residence at Paris, in preparation for a return to the seminary of Châlons. But the result of this move was other than he then contemplated; it was not his fate to become a professor in a Catholic seminary.

It was in 1881—in his twenty-fifth year—that Loisy returned to Paris as both student and, later on, professor; Duchesne opened the way for him by obtaining for him the post of repetitor in Hebrew. Meanwhile he followed the lectures of Duchesne on early Church history, and of Vigouroux on Scripture. At that time, he says: 'I had read no heterodox writer, and I had hardly any acquaintance with Biblical rationalism save through its refutation as set before us by M. Vigouroux.'[2]

In a note of March 8th, 1882, he wrote:

On one side we find routine asserting itself as tradition; on the other novelty making claim to be truth. The first is no more representative of faith than is the second a reliable presentation of science. These two spirits are at war in the Biblical domain, and I ask myself if there is anyone on earth capable of holding the right balance between faith and science. Were there such an one, he would be my master.[3]

Further on he wrote:

I have no guide for this *via media*; at least I think not, and in saying so I do not think I am too distrustful of this one or the other. I must simply be guided by Providence.

He goes on with a prayer:

O my God, give me twenty years of health, patience and labour, with such a spirit of discernment, sincerity and humility as will permit Christian science to advance without danger for

---

[1] *Mém.* 1, 84.   [2] *Idem*, p. 102.
[3] *Idem*, p. 102.

the learned, and for the edification of the Church and the confusion of her enemies.[1]

In recording those notes he calls special attention to that phrase: 'I have no guide.' Of course it was not, as he adds, M. Vigouroux who could be that guide—but what about Duchesne? Duchesne, one of the greatest living scholars? Duchesne, who believed in him and encouraged him? Duchesne, who was not indeed occupied with direct questions of Scripture but who was well aware of the general position of the Catholic Church in its regard? Why not Duchesne?

Strangely enough, had Loisy at that stage accepted Duchesne as his mentor, he would probably have followed a safer path from the ecclesiastical point of view; he would probably have also followed a more prosperous and successful path through life.

But, stranger still, it was, as it clearly appears to me from his notes of that period, that it was his attachment to his faith, his still ardent loyalty to the Church, that prevented him from putting himself under the direction of a man like Duchesne, whose mind did not respond to his own from the religious stand-point; a man not ready to venture all in the cause of religion and truth.

In our intimate relations Duchesne showed himself other than he appeared in his letters. The end which I set before myself in my exegetical work was not quite the same as that which he sought in his works on ecclesiastical history. I knew well that he had much yet to teach me in the order of science; but my life was consecrated not to science but to the service of the Church through science. I think it is certain that I was following the star that I beheld during my seminary life...; the star was more brilliant, the horizon was wider, the way more complicated and difficult, but the direction was the same. And I think it has not varied even since I have learned to count less on the Church for the moral progress of mankind.

I soon realized that Duchesne did not enter into these my spiritual dispositions, which were the best part of me, and that

[1] *Mém.* I, 103.

his closer acquaintance would injure rather than benefit them. The Voltairean tone which he affected, even more in his conversation than in his writings, did not please me at all; I thought it showed, not only a lack of good taste, but also a lack of the moral sense. Nor did I inwardly appreciate his Rabelaisian jokes. It seemed to me, in fact, and I began to see it more and more, that if Duchesne was a wonderful torch-bearer on special questions, he lacked depth, and did not even care to see too far into general and fundamental subjects. I even thought that, though he took pleasure in casting light within the limits that I have indicated, he was in no hurry to compromise himself in the service of truth; that while he clearly realized the intellectual poverty of Roman Catholicism, he was only disposed to seek a remedy in so far as there was no risk to his own career. He foresaw for himself a brilliant scientific future in the *Institut de France*, and it was his ambition to attain this future without... using his strength in reconciling the antagonism between science, which was his chief interest, and the theological tradition of the Church, whose intransigence he deemed, with some reason, insuperable. He aimed no more at defending the faith of the Church than at modernizing it. He has contributed more than anyone to release a scientific movement in French Catholicism without troubling as to the result. Like a great sailor he trimmed his sails to the tempest....

To avert misunderstanding, I will add that no man can make an absolute pronouncement on the secret of another. Being convinced that Duchesne, during the years of our intimacy, did not understand my interior sentiments...it would be rash to claim that I understood him from the first. I will only say what I have said, and what I know: Duchesne appeared to me more and more, as I knew him, a very solid *savant*, and a rather superficial believer.[1]

Later on he tells us he declined the offer of Duchesne to accompany him on a journey, for apart from questions of health

I had another reason, which I could not avow, and that he never seemed to suspect; for, as I have hinted above, I did not want him to exercise an assimilating influence over me, and while I appreciated his friendship and kindness I avoided

[1] *Mém.* I, 105–106.

a close intimacy which would have drawn me into his moral orbit.[1]

I imagine that some will say that it reads rather strangely, this account, from the man who left the Church, of his dissatisfaction, from the religious point of view, with the man who stayed in it. But this would be a superficial criticism. What Loisy objected to was any lack of seriousness in such questions. So long as he believed in the Church, he did not like another believer to regard the relations of the Church with science as negligible, and, still more, as matter of joke.

Furthermore, Loisy's mind was of a supremely positive character, and he was, I think, unable to understand the type of mind that does, really, combine genuine faith with a vein of underlying scepticism. Duchesne had something of the spirit of Bishop Blougram:

> With me faith means perpetual unbelief
> Kept quiet like the snake 'neath Michael's foot.[2]

And, like Bishop Blougram, Duchesne could give rein to his wit; could mock and joke, and could do it all over one of these *plantureux déjeuners* which did not accord with the ascetic disposition of his friend.

But the second reason, as I gather from the *Mémoires*, for a lessening of intimacy between these two men was that Duchesne regarded the subject of Scriptural exegesis as hopelessly dangerous from the ecclesiastical point of view; whereas for Loisy it was the supreme question.

I remember (he writes) a talk that I had with Duchesne on this subject during a walk in the *Jardin des Plantes* towards the end of May, 1889, about a fortnight before our conversation of June 11th, which closed our relations for some years. The decision regarding the chair of Holy Scripture was not yet made, and we were discussing the matter, though I was already determined to accept the proposition of Mgr d'Hulst if it were maintained. Duchesne was opposed to my acceptance. He

---

[1] *Mém.* 1, 113.
[2] One might almost imagine Duchesne as the model of Browning's great bishop.

was already developing the idea, to which he adhered more and more after our separation, of the moral impossibility of a scientific evolution of Biblical exegesis in the Roman Church. He insisted on the permanent, and already imminent, danger to which I should expose myself by assuming the responsibility of a teaching that was sure to bring me into conflict with theologians. He pointed out to me further, as he had often done before, with what ease I could pursue an honourable career in the domain of Semitic philology, with the prospect of that Paradise of the learned, a chair in the Institute.[1]

Duchesne was abundantly right, as regarded both the danger and the disadvantage of the work in question, but the contrary attractions were not of a kind to weigh with his friend.

It should be noted that von Hügel, also, was distressed by Duchesne's detachment from the Biblical question. Thus on May 6th, 1895, he wrote to Loisy that he was pained and astonished by the apparent determination of Duchesne not to enter on such questions, nor to encourage others. And on February 6th, 1896, he writes from Rome that he finds him little sympathetic with the work of others except with that of Loisy himself and also resolute to avoid Scripture questions.

I seldom see him but he enters on the subject, and tries to convert me to the idea that there is nothing to do but to wait.[2]

These then seem to me the two fundamental causes of disagreement between the two men; the one too cynical, the other too serious; the one too cautious and ambitious, the other too detached and uncalculating.

Unhappily, too, a sense of personal affront entered into their last relations at this time. The story may be read in the *Mémoires* as in *Choses Passées*. Loisy had counted on Duchesne to obtain him a chair at the 'École des Hautes Études', and he considered that Duchesne had let him down and not fulfilled his promises. Here we touch on a personal controversy with which this study is not concerned; and once personal considerations entered, with the resulting possibility of misunderstanding and offence, it is probable that a good deal

[1] *Mém.* I, 164.   [2] *Idem*, p. 396.

might be said in defence of Duchesne and in criticism of Loisy.

I subjoin the following letter, which I received from Loisy on the death of Duchesne:

May 14th, 1922.

Dear Miss Petre,

The death of Duchesne was rapid, but physically he had been getting sensibly weaker for some time. He had continually asked to be replaced at Rome, because he wished to spend his last days in France. Von Hügel told me he had received a very sad letter from him at the beginning of the year. I met him for the last time in 1917, and found him much aged. His life as a savant was magnificent, and could perhaps have been greater still, and certainly more peaceful, had he not been of the Church. The prevailing sentiment of ecclesiastical authority in his respect was always one of suspicion, a suspicion that often checked his scientific activity. He himself took pains to avoid any scandal. It is none the less regrettable that the publication of the fourth volume of his 'Ancient History of the Church' has been so long delayed. The publisher will now, I expect, bring it out without troubling about the *Imprimatur* or the Index. You may have seen that Duchesne forbade any speech at his funeral; he was, no doubt, suspicious of his panegyrists. The official laudation has not been wanting in the French press, with a wilful disregard of his situation in regard to the Church. For the rest, silence has already fallen until he is spoken of again when his panegyric is pronounced by his successor at the French Academy.

. . . .

CHAPTER IV

VON HÜGEL

ONE can never witness the disintegration of a friendship without a sense of sorrow. Loisy was not fortunate in this respect, and as we have seen his relations with Duchesne quickly diminish in cordiality and confidence, so we now approach the story of his connection with von Hügel; a much sadder story in its ending, because of the pain on both sides, though perhaps even more inevitable given the characters of the two men.

Von Hügel always betrayed his Foreign Office heredity, and, in some sense, Loisy always betrayed his agricultural descent. Von Hügel was a seeker after truth, and he was also a propagandist; it was in his propaganda that he displayed diplomatic characteristics of which Loisy had not the embryo. Loisy acted, whether in his search for truth, or in its utterance, with the directness of a farm labourer in his work on the soil. He was not incapable of artifice, but he did not attempt to manipulate the minds and actions of others. Von Hügel could be oppressive—he was, in Italian sense, something of a *prepotente*—but he was never vindictive; Loisy was not oppressive, but, though not vindictive, was keenly resentful of direct opposition, unforgiving, and apt to brood over slights and offences. His *Mémoires* testify to his sensitiveness and inability to endure contradiction patiently.

Von Hügel was indefatigable in the service of a friend so long as that friend was serving the cause in which he believed; and though he never wholly abandoned anyone, nor renounced the claims of old friendship, he quickly cooled when his friends took an independent line which he deemed injurious to their common cause. And one mistake which he made was that he thought they had a common cause when, in fact, their aims were not quite the same as his, or still more, he failed to per-

ceive that his own aims were far more clearly cut and definite
than those of many with whom he first worked. For he had a
German thoroughness of plan, and each of us was expected
to take his part towards the fulfilment of that plan. But many,
in that time of religious crisis in which he and his leading
friends first came together, had no such defined plan; they were
pushing their way through unknown forests of the mind; they
knew they had to get through, but they did not know what
they would find at the end of their journey. Hence they were
impatient of checks and regulations which were reasonable
enough for the fulfilment of a definite policy, but which were
irritating to men who were in the full tide of battle and could
not yet see their way.

Then, again, von Hügel was cautious, and he was also correct. Loisy was, on the whole, correct, but he was only
cautious in detail, not in his general policy; and Tyrrell, of
course, was neither cautious nor correct.

And so we find von Hügel and Loisy starting on a campaign
far more tragic in its cause and issue than either of them, and
von Hügel less than Loisy, foresaw at the time.

The first connection of the two men was made by way of
letter. Von Hügel was ever on the watch for minds that were
moving forward in the study of religious questions; he had
immense patience with slow movers, but ardently supported
the bolder pioneers. He was, in fact, a liaison officer between
religious thinkers, and this is why it is so absurd to endeavour
to discharge him from responsibility in the Modernist movement.

Loisy heard from him, for the first time, in a letter of April
30th, 1893, wherein he tells him how he has followed his
writings, and how he is actively propagating them.[1] Shortly
afterwards Loisy was dismissed from the *Institut Catholique*; and
from that time von Hügel followed, with keen sympathy, the
vicissitudes of his friend's life, defending him, and even endeavouring to protect him, so far as lay in his power. Thus he
wrote, in May 1901, a letter to Cardinal Rampolla, in which

[1] *Mém.* I, 287.

he boldly pointed out the bad effect that would be produced
on the thinking world, by a condemnation of the works of a
man like Loisy.[1] And he unflinchingly risked compromising
himself, along with his friend, when he declined to take part
in a Roman Society for the study of Biblical questions, because

I must wait to see what is going to happen to my friend.
I should be acting a lie if, by my humble presence, I gave
rise to the belief that the work [of such a society] was serious,
when there was possibility of the suppression of light and air
by such a condemnation.

And Loisy answers:

I should certainly not have been as patient and persevering
in defending myself as you have been in protecting me from a
condemnation which would do most harm to its own authors.[2]

And much later, in 1913, when there was no longer the same
mutual understanding, he crossed swords with Dean Inge on
behalf of both Loisy and Tyrrell.[3]

Much more might be said on this point; but my aim is
simply to indicate the part, a generous part, that von Hügel
took in the destiny of his friend during the first years of their
acquaintance.

But the diplomatic and temporizing quality of his mind was
soon to make itself felt. At bottom he always cared more for
the cause than for the persons who took part in it; an attitude
of mind which we expect in political matters, but which is
more questionable in religious ones. This characteristic it was
that made him often urge his collaborators into dangerous
positions, though he was distressed if they afterwards advanced
beyond the point at which he aimed. Thus Loisy recounts an
incident in the early years of their friendship, when von Hügel
asked Mgr Mignot to intervene with the Pope on behalf of
Loisy. Loisy remarks: 'It was asking a good deal.'[4] And
many, more marked, examples, might be cited, on this point,
in the lives of others as well as that of Loisy.

[1] *Mém.* II, 41.
[3] *Idem,* III, 270–271.
[2] *Idem,* II, 71.
[4] *Idem,* I, 296.

In his policy with persons von Hügel was rather like a chess player; he planned out each move; but when the pieces showed that they were alive and self-moving he became anxious and solicitous lest his plan of campaign should come to nought.

And so, quite early, we note, between these two men, the germs of a disagreement that was eventually to cool their friendship, even though it was never wholly quenched; a disagreement that even passed into tacit hostility.

Having had precisely the same advice offered by von Hügel to myself on one occasion, I was interested to note that, as early as 1894, he advised his friend to be silent and disappear for a time because 'the Pope could not live for ever'. Loisy replied that he in no way agreed as to 'the necessity of his own absolute disappearance'.[1]

Later on he resented the Baron's advice—which was almost an injunction—not to publish an apology, which he had contemplated writing, but had not yet written: 'I never liked', he says, 'that anyone should, so imperatively, prescribe my line of conduct.'[2]

And soon we may note the first appearance of a phantom which haunted von Hügel to the end of his life in his relations with several of his friends; the phantom dread that they were reducing the reality of God; were forgetting His transcendence by an exaggerated doctrine of immanence.

The first occasion on which we may note the emergence of this fear arose in regard to the philosophy of the Immanentist Marcel Hébert. He wrote, on September 2nd, 1902, that he was suffering from the apparent toleration accorded to this philosophy by both Loisy and Mgr Mignot.[3] On this point we shall see more presently.

On June 1st, 1900, an article by Loisy, over the signature Després, occasioned an interchange of views between the two friends which is particularly symptomatic. In this article Loisy discussed the significance of the Pope's Encyclical *Providentissimus* on Biblical studies.

[1] *Mém.* I, 341.   [2] *Idem*, II, 105.
[3] *Idem*, II, 131.

The Baron was displeased with its tone and a discussion ensued, a year and a half later, on the matter of its reimpression. Von Hügel considered it bitter and unpractical and he then passed on to a kind of prophetical statement of what he regarded as Loisy's rightful work and mission.

In fifty years' time, he thought, the historian would distinguish two main lines of Loisy's work: first, his work upon "historico-critical" and "philosophico-apologetic" problems, in which a clear and powerful course of development could be traced; and second, his attempt to establish a place for himself in a world which threatened to destroy him. The historian would find it hard either to follow this second line or to relate it to the first. Von Hügel, in his defence of Loisy, identified himself with the first.[1]

It must be admitted that such a judgment was not soothing or encouraging to one who had endeavoured to render religious doctrine spiritually immune from historic difficulties. His second line of work was not, he maintains, useless if the Church had been willing to listen to reason; it presented 'a means of transition, a bridge between theology and science, an attempt at such a transition as would maintain the spiritual essence of dogma'; and he believes that his attempt has not been wholly futile, and that there are, perhaps, devout souls who have been helped by it.[2]

And such policy is, he indicates, to some extent that of the Baron himself. Thus:

We know that he himself treats pontifical directions with extreme diplomacy, veiling and twisting what he finds deplorable, while refusing to admit their absurdity, nor allowing himself to see it.[3]

There is certainly a contradiction between the Baron's attitude as set forth above, and his ardent propaganda for *L'Évangile et l'Église*, and the difference can only be explained as resulting from his belief that the incriminated article was impolitic and provocative and bad strategy. But a thrust such as he

---

[1] *Mém.* II, 180.   [2] *Idem*, p. 182.   [3] *Idem*, p. 180.

inflicted here, and repeated on later occasions, went too deep to be easily forgiven. For although, as Loisy admits on this same occasion, he was not saying, in these attempts at apology, all that could be said; although those attempts were not devoid of subtlety, and might later seem only half sincere, they were not made in his character of historian.

And, actually, it was not the subtlety or reserve to which von Hügel objected; he was himself subtle and reserved; he objected in so far as these writings did not conform to the scheme he had in view; and also, most certainly, in so far as there was any accent of bitterness or revolt in the same article. For nothing would have changed von Hügel into a rebel; he was in the Church and he intended to remain in it; and none of us knew what conditions he may have eventually had to fulfil in order to remain faithful to this purpose. No one can say what might have been the religious outcome if von Hügel's first friends had ranged themselves under his banner, and fought according to his directions; it is an interesting speculation. Perhaps the result would have been a policy of appeasement on the part of the Church; perhaps, on the contrary, von Hügel himself would have been the first to be decapitated, in spite of his loyal intentions.

The Baron's faithful attachment to the Church, and his definite conception of the right policy to follow, make his steady perseverance on behalf of his friend the more admirable. For even when Loisy, having incurred the major excommunication, had become a *vitandus*, von Hügel did not give him up. But gradually the river of years that parted them grew wider as it approached the sea; and it was the memory of their friendship, and not its reality, that remained.

As I remarked above, the question of Divine transcendency, as against Immanentism, began to obsess the Baron's mind to such point as certainly to produce misunderstanding on the part of other friends as well as of Loisy. In his *Mémoires* the latter quotes, in particular, a letter of the Baron to Prof. René Guiran, of July 11th, 1921.[1] In it he does, indeed, as Loisy

[1] See *Selected Letters*, p. 333.

says,[1] make short work of a good many of his former friends, who have, to his mind, failed, some more, some less, on this vital point. Thus he indicts first Loisy, then Tyrrell, then Buonaiuti and Minocchi (an assembly of names in itself misleading and undiscriminating); and lastly even Blondel and Laberthonnière—his early oracles, whom he had, first of all, introduced to so many. (I may mention that it was from him that I came to know the *Dogmatisme Moral* of Laberthonnière.)

In his judgment of most of these men he was both prejudiced and unjust; the question of Immanentism had become a positive obsession; and, from my own acquaintance with von Hügel, I can fully endorse Loisy's judgment on the point. And it seems to me that von Hügel was, to a great extent, reacting against his own previous convictions and attitude. He had dipped on the side of Immanentism further than he judged right in his later developments; and he was, unconsciously, stripping himself of the influences of those early days, and exaggerating the views of those who had thus influenced him. The last meeting of these two men was at Garnay, where Loisy was then living, in April 1906. He wrote to Loisy after his return to London, and Loisy thus remarks on this letter, and describes his own feelings:

There was a touching page on the feelings which seized him when we separated on a country road...as he was going on to take the train to Paris. Neither of us knew it, but we were not destined to meet again, and we were both going on to a future that would upset all our forecasts.[2]

I add to this study of their relations the letter I received from Loisy on the death of von Hügel and a letter on the question which had divided them.

January 31*st*, 1925.

I was greatly touched by your letter. Miss Hildegarde had sent me a telegram on Tuesday which I received at the end of the day. Naturally the telegram contained but few words: 'My father died peacefully this morning.' It was all that was needed since I could not have gone to the funeral, besides

---

[1] *Mém.* III, 403.   [2] *Idem*, II, 516.

which the participation at any Catholic ceremony is prohibited to a notorious excommunicate.

Yes indeed, it is a part of our past that is gone. He was with us for long years with all his love and devotion. He did not forget it, but he had assumed towards the survivors of the tragic enterprise an attitude of displeasure which was not true to his character, nor, if I may say so, to his graciousness. It was always to me as inexplicable as painful to find in him not only dogmatic intransigence, but even the painful tone of orthodox controversialists. On the part of so deep and sincere a mystic this astonished me. I fancy that his director, Abbé Huvelin, would have reminded him on such occasions that the only sentiment which should animate the friends of God, in their dealings with any human beings whatsoever, was charity. He seemed to bear us a grudge for not following his line, though it was as impossible for us to do so as for him to follow ours. He might have seen this. But I cannot but think that his health was seriously compromised from the date of the great crisis in 1907, and that there was something of the sick man in the rigid orthodoxy which he displayed, an orthodoxy which, given the exigencies of Rome, must have been less real than sincere; and in the kind of resentment he manifested for those who followed another course. I am certain that, had he been more himself, he would have been always simply and perfectly good to us, even if he did not approve of us entirely.

There were two recent circumstances in which the strangeness of his attitude was particularly evident to me.

1. You remember the article he wrote on Duchesne about three years ago, in which he cited a letter in which Duchesne boasted that he had never been lured by the chimeras of Tyrrell, Houtin and Loisy. Quite vainly I tried to make him see how imprudent and displeasing was this quotation. For if this article had appeared in a French periodical I should have been obliged to oppose to it the letters that Duchesne wrote me after the publication of *L'Évangile et l'Église* and *Autour d'un petit livre*; I might even add what he wrote me in 1917, after my little book *La Religion*. What Duchesne thought of Modernism may be said in two words—'Vain effort'.

2. Last September the Baron learned from Dom Wilmart that I had been made a 'chevalier de la légion d'honneur', and he wrote to congratulate me, but he added that, as a Catholic, he was bound to feel a certain anxiety over anything

that increased my importance. What could I answer? I was obliged to say that I was in no way greater, and that he could ask my French friends, Brémond for instance, if my presence in the domain of higher teaching could be considered as a calamity for the Church. It seemed to me that he, otherwise so delicate, hardly realized how such words could wound.

And now that he has entered into eternal rest, we must only remember the good that he did, the good that he wished to do, and the friend that he had been for us and many others.

Paris, March 8th, 1930.

I am glad that you were interested in my little preface. I read with the greatest interest your discussion on the existence of God according to von Hügel. It seems to me that you have analysed his thought with great exactitude and the evolution of his thought on the subject. This is important.

I may tell you that what has most struck me in von Hügel is the anguish that this question occasioned him. You know also that for my part, without regarding this question with indifference, or denial, or misunderstanding, I can also face it without trouble, and can refuse to dogmatize in the matter. The very example of von Hügel would induce me to adopt this position. I am not obliged to affirm beyond what I can see. It seems to me that with regard to the problem of the universe the greatest doctor or philosopher might well know little more than an ant or a worm; I mean from the point of view of the infinite. On the other hand the consideration of human misery, which is great indeed, encourages me to think that our race can do much for its improvement and that some instinct urges it. Let us help it, let us work with it, in its own best direction, with its own best representatives, putting aside false pretexts and divisions. There is a realization of God to be sought in humanity, and this is the realization to which humanity aspires.

Who leads us? A question almost blasphemous, or at any rate without significance. If there were a *who*, it would be humanity; but it is not humanity because humanity does not walk of itself, it is not a living liberty. Well, then, there is no *who* measurable by its yard-stick. It is nevertheless a fact that this arrogant vermin is solidary with the planet that bears it and with the whole universe, of which it is part, contained and continuing. But that with which humanity is solidary and on which it is dependent is not someone as occupied with it as it is with itself. Is it capable of sounding and understanding and defining Him? It may have thought so, but what presumption! It is, in fact, relatively more easy for humanity to know itself without reasoning so much, than to enclose the absolute in syllogisms. Some intellectual and moral asceticism would not be amiss before reconstructing a metaphysic, if the wish to do so should return. To save the future of humanity on the planet might be a more noble occupation if it could understand and undertake it, and it might be the only labour that would please the Eternal, if He deigned to regard it.

Forgive me for having plunged into metaphysics, but it is your fault.

CHAPTER V

THE MODERNIST MOVEMENT

I ALWAYS employ the term *Modernism* with a sense of inner protest, because it has been given a denominational character which it never possessed. The Pope described it as a congeries of heresies; and this, from the point of view of the Encyclical, was a far truer estimate. The different paths eventually followed, by those who were classed together at the beginning, is proof enough that the movement was in no way sectarian. However, one has to take the term as usually understood; and though Loisy never ranged himself with any party, we have to study that phase of his life in which he was, to some extent, associated with other so-called Modernists. He was not fond of going back on that period of his life; and he once said to me that it made him feel as though he were 'raking his own ashes'. Still, his writings played a considerable part in the movement, and are certainly essential to his own history.

I think we might sum up the purpose and significance of those writings as expressing his last *hopeful* effort on behalf of the Church. After that his apologetic efforts came to an end, and, however much some of us may regret it, the fact cannot be denied. I firmly believe that, in his much later works, another form of apologetic emerged; but of that we will not speak here.

I said his last *hopeful* effort; and it is in its character of hope that those writings may be classed with others of the Modernist movement. For, if there was any real bond of union between these widely differing men, it was the common quality of *hope*; hope that the Church would not repudiate the truths of science and history; hope that their own labours might conduce to this cause; hope, more than hope, that the spiritual essence of dogma would survive all assaults of unbelieving criticism; hope in the indestructibility of faith and its capacity for the absorption of all human truth and knowledge.

Very different was the form which this hope assumed in the minds of the different men who cherished it. Loisy's aim was to open the eyes of theologians to the existence of the historic problem; to put Catholic students abreast of others in exegetical questions. He wanted freedom in his historical and critical studies; freedom to pursue them without hindrance, and to teach without equivocation. His main object was not apologetic, but he was drawn to an apologetic attempt by the impact of history on Scriptural science and belief. The present generation can scarcely conceive the effect on traditional belief of the—almost sudden—emergence of a new historic conception of the documents of Christianity. When one considers that even the mind of Newman seems to have had no suspicion or foreboding of the impending crisis, no conception of the coming devastation of faith that was to be wrought by historical criticism, it may be imagined how little the ordinary believer was prepared for the storm.

Those who saw what was coming and endeavoured to prepare for it, as against those who were blind to the danger, were somewhat akin to the corresponding parties in the political world; those who foretell coming danger and those who deny it.

In 1896 we have a first hint of Loisy's most celebrated apologetic effort, that which took shape in *L'Évangile et l'Église*. The question of Anglican Orders was a burning one at the time, and in his correspondence with von Hügel he refers to a work he had in view, which would have had some bearing on the question, but continues as follows:

I am going further in my dreams. My catechisms of perseverance have given me the idea of a general exposition of Catholic doctrine for the end of this century, something useful for everyone and conciliating for those outside the Church.

He goes on to ask about Newman, from whom he thinks he can get some help in this design, and 'if only I can live four years I want to die a Father of the Church'.[1]

In September 1926 he came on the work which he had

---

[1] *Mém.* I, 410.

planned and partly executed at the time when he wrote, as
above, to von Hügel. Of it he then writes:

The first sketch shows that the fundamental and dominating
idea of the whole work was the reform of the intellectual system
of the Catholic Church; neither more nor less; and all the rest,
criticism, history, philosophy, social considerations, were to be
ordered to this end. It was much, and more than could be
realized by one man, or several, in the course of a generation.
But I did not feel quite alone; I did not expect immediate
success; I did not know when or how I should publish my
essay.[1]

He goes on to say:

What I did not foresee was that this enterprise would almost
inevitably lead me away from Catholicism. Ever since 1893
I knew that there was risk; but that the risk would be fatal
I only understood in 1903, after the condemnation of *L'Évangile
et l'Église*.[2]

If my readers will accept my suggestion that the characteristic of Modernism, in which all so-called Modernists were
united, was hopefulness, then this unpublished work may
certainly be classed as his greatest Modernist effort; wider and
more ambitious than *L'Évangile et l'Église*. And he ceased to
be Modernist when he gave up the attempt to bring about a
new life in the intellectual system of the Church; but he ceased
also to be a Modernist when he ceased to be a Catholic.

Von Hügel, on the contrary, ceased to be a Modernist when
he did not cease to be a Catholic, but when he closed, to a
large extent, his intellectual efforts for a broader policy on the
part of the Church; and when he no longer stimulated his
friends or followers, but rather endeavoured to check and
control them. With him, too, it was when he gave up hope
that he gave up Modernism. I must not let these words be
misunderstood. I do not mean that he gave up hope in the
Church; very much the contrary. But I cannot but see that
he did quite give up hope in the effort which he had fostered
amongst others, and in which he had himself taken a leading

[1] *Mém.* I, 443.   [2] *Idem.*

part, to obtain Church tolerance, if not recognition, of the results of science and history.

I think that it is from the pages of what he terms the *Livre Inédit* that we can best obtain what we may call the Modernist programme of Loisy. The word itself only came into vogue with the Encyclical *Pascendi* of 1907; but the deeds or misdeeds with which that document dealt dated ten to twenty years earlier. The work to which I refer belongs to the years 1897–1898.[1] In its introduction he says:

We are witnesses of a complete transformation of religious science, and theology would be wrong to neglect it on the pretext that it knows beforehand what to answer. Let theologians remember the case of Galileo...history and criticism may have their own Galileos, against whom theological criticisms and censures may prove vain....A science of religion is taking shape outside Catholicism and in opposition to it. To neutralize the dangerous influence of this science, over which there is no exterior control, to prevent its spread amongst a public that can read and write, we need a religious science in and for the Church.

In a very significant passage he states what is to be expected by a Catholic critic, namely a twofold distrust, first on the part of the theologian, next on the part of the scientist:

He has to reduce their opposition to its proper limits, repudiating in science only what can be repudiated, only its unjust claims; having no doubt as to the fate which awaits his effort at conciliation, which will be contradiction mingled with surprise, and mitigated only by the fear that he may be more right than they dare to admit—this as regards the reaction of those apologists who regard themselves as the official defenders of tradition; contradiction also on the part of critics, who will maintain that while the Catholicism he defends may be defensible, it is not true Catholicism.

These last words are important. So long as Loisy maintained, against such criticism, that it was, indeed, true Catholicism that he was defending, he could be termed a Modernist and

[1] In the quotations that follow I translate freely. For reference see *Mémoires*, Vol. I, Chap. XVI *passim*.

also a Catholic. When he abandoned this position, he abandoned his faith in the Church as well as his interest in the Modernist cause; which was the cause of von Hügel, Tyrrell, Archbishop Mignot (in his measure) and many others. For there was then, in those early days, a certain union between men who were destined to part company later; and it was that united effort which can be truly termed Modernist.

And in abandoning Modernism Loisy eventually abandoned Catholicism, for it was only Catholicism, as conciliable with the march of human knowledge and science, to which he could in sincerity adhere.

All the same, as the story goes on, too long a story to give in all its details, but of which the salient points must be presented, we may be led to ask ourselves whether, with different treatment on the part of ecclesiastical authority, he might not have found some *locus standi*. For, after all, our possession of truth is always limited, and often obscure; Loisy believed to the end in religion as the essential moral and spiritual factor of life, and he also believed in Christianity as far its noblest presentation; he even believed in the Church in so far as she was its principal organ; and he might possibly, without insincerity, have kept his place in her, rejoicing, as he always did, in the faith of the simple and leaving the intransigent schools to find their own level. This is a 'might have been', but not a wholly absurd one.

To return to the *Livre Inédit*.

This work is not one of learned history, of profound philosophy, of transcendental theology, or triumphant apologetic, but a gentle mixture of all these, and a sincere expression of the contemporary religious problem as the author sees it. . . . He desires to show, not only the permanent solution that Catholicism offers of the religious problem, but the necessity of following a certain course in order to realize this end more perfectly. . . .

My last chapter will be an estimate, hopeful and confident, of the past and future of Catholicism.[1]

The *Livre Inédit* became a kind of store-house, from which he drew material for articles. In it he planned chapters on

[1] *Mém.* i, 446–7.

Jesus Christ, the Gospel and the Church, the Gospel and dogma, the Gospel and worship, the Intellectual régime of the Church, Science and Faith, Religion and Life, etc. etc.[1]

Of it he wrote to the Baron, June 21st, 1897:

> Do not talk of my great work; it will perhaps never exist. I am convinced that, for eighteen centuries, no apologist has had either greater difficulties or a greater measure of good-will than myself.[2]

The *Livre Inédit* goes on to summarize four theories of religious faith—the Catholic absolutist; the rationalistic as presented by Renan; the Protestant-Liberal (which he criticized definitely in *L'Évangile et l'Église*); and the theory of Christian development, according to Newman. It was the last that served him in this apologetic effort. But, as he remarks, it would first be necessary to get theologians to accept the very principle of evolution, which was directly contrary to their conception of an absolute revelation and an ecclesiastical imperialism.[3] But

> The purpose of Christianity is not the domination of the Church over mankind, but the salvation of men through the Church.[4]

Summing up the fate of this unpublished book, he says:

> Such it was; a true summary of what Catholic Modernism ought to be . . . it failed in its end; it would have failed even had it been published *in toto*. But I think I may say that the Church, in disappointing my hopes, ruined the faith I had in her; or rather forced me to plant my faith elsewhere.[5]

This *Livre Inédit* was, in its whole, the work of a soul even more than a mind; I mean that it was the utterance of his spiritual and apostolic aspirations; that it was an endeavour to use his knowledge, his judgment, his intellect for the enlightenment of his own religious body. He knew the perils to faith, for he was conscious of them in his own inner life; but he knew too that such perils must be surmounted if the Church was to survive, and he believed that the dangers could be met,

---

[1] *Mém.* I, 439. [2] *Idem.* [3] *Idem*, pp. 448–449.
[4] *Idem*, p. 473. [5] *Idem*, p. 477.

and the Church could outlive this storm as she had outlived others, but in virtue of adaptation and not intransigence.

But meanwhile things were not going easily for him. We must remember how new to Catholic students was the most rudimentary notion of strictly scientific exegesis in regard to the Scriptures. There had been sporadic appearances of criticism, but such had been quickly forgotten, and the Bible had been regarded as immune from secular handling. Amongst Catholics this immunity was preserved by the Church; it was both the proof and the source of her teaching. Amongst Protestants the Scriptures were sacrosanct as the Word of God, and no further proof was needed. Had critics and historians never turned their attention to these sacred documents these two positions might have been indefinitely maintained; in which case the faith of many might not have been troubled, but, on the other hand, that same faith would have rested, in so far as the Scriptures were concerned, on an insecure foundation, that might have given way much more fatally than by timely research and criticism. For nothing can live in complete isolation, and artificial immunity would eventually have resulted in spiritual impoverishment. By the unbeliever criticism was welcomed as a destroying factor; by the Catholic believer, such as Loisy, it was regarded as fresh pabulum for the elucidation of dogma and faith—a problem indeed, and an arduous one, but, since all truth was one, it could not be fatal unless faith was void—unless the Church could no longer absorb the growing knowledge of mankind.

As this is not a history of the life of Loisy, but a study of his religious significance, I will not attempt a detailed account of his final rupture with the Church; all this may be read in his *Mémoires*, Vol. II. I will content myself with the mention of a few leading events.

On December 28th, 1900, he had an interview with Cardinal Richard, Archbishop of Paris, one who was largely instrumental in all that led to his condemnation. The Cardinal told him that his articles were causing disturbance amongst Catholics. Loisy remarked, *inter alia*, that the very fact of his

contesting the historical character of certain chapters of the
Bible removed those chapters from the possibility of historical
error, since they were thus established as containing something
other than history. When accused of being too much influenced
by German critics, he replied that it was the work of Catholic
apologists, with their reticence and inexactitude, that had
chiefly troubled him.[1]

In a letter to Father Lepidi, a Roman official, and Master
of the Sacred Palace, 1901, he says:

I have tried to show that the certain or probable evidence
of criticism and history can be reconciled with the principles
of Catholic doctrine, or, rather, how from history thus renewed
a favourable testimony to the supernatural reality of revelation
can be drawn....Very Rev. Father, I have not in me the
making of a heresiarch or even a heretic. During the twenty-
two years of my priesthood I have served the Church with all
the devotion of which I am capable.... I do not speak of the
moral trials I have endured, for I am not writing to complain
or to accuse anybody.[2]

In a letter to von Hügel of November 25th, 1901, he says:

You are the true Father of the Church, the true Augustine;
I am something of a Jerome, which I own with shame.

He has before him the choice of intellectual suicide, or
untruth, which latter might assure him an honourable position
in the Church. Actually he is an object of suspicion both to
the Church and to the learned outside the Church.

I do what I can, and I grieve that the Church has not used
me and will not use me in her service.[3]

The year 1902 witnessed the publication of *L'Évangile et
l'Église*, almost the best known of Loisy's works; a definite
apologetic effort; a refutation of the Liberal Protestant Christological doctrine as set forth by Adolf Harnack; a partial
adaptation of Newman's doctrine of development; and an
almost categorical statement of faith in Catholicism along with
recognition of the claims of history. There is a sad irony in

[1] *Mém.* II, 14–16.   [2] *Idem*, pp. 38–39.   [3] *Idem*, p. 72.

the thought that it was an effort to defend the faith, to help those who were troubled by the emergence of the historic problem, that hastened his condemnation, rather than his strictly scientific, and less religious, works. The injustice meted out to this work by many Catholics was perhaps capped by one Catholic writer who termed it a *hoax*! Much bitter suffering and labour had gone to the making of a work which aimed at being a testimony both to faith and science.

Personally I cannot help regretting that the *Livre Inédit*, from which this later work was in part drawn, did not appear in its own character and clothing. He himself thinks that the controversial character of *L'Évangile et l'Église* somewhat altered its purpose. However, it must be taken as it stands, and its significance was such that it was republished as late as 1929. Of this book he says, after a reference to Harnack's *Wesen des Christentums*, which he regarded as 'the essence of Liberal Protestantism':

I thought it opportune to sketch a history of Christian development from the Gospel onwards, to show that the essence of the Gospel, in so far as an essence existed, had been truly perpetuated in Catholic Christianity, and that the transformations of the Gospel in Catholicism had been something other than decadence and progressive alteration.[1]

On this point it is interesting to note that Wilfrid Ward, one of the closest students of Newman, wrote to von Hügel that the author 'showed a consummate knowledge of Newman's aim and tendency, while, at the same time, both extending and limiting the domain of Catholic evolution'.[2]

This work was, as we have seen, an apologetic effort, but it was an effort whose value could not be estimated without some knowledge and acceptance of the process of history and criticism. It was, like all his work of that period, like, indeed, the work of von Hügel, of Tyrrell and others, a statement of the impregnability of Catholic doctrine in its spiritual significance, along with a fearless recognition of historical

[1] *Mém.* ii, 167. [2] *Idem*, p. 173.

facts. But its apologetic value was ignored, and its historic admissions were condemned. On January 17th, 1903, Cardinal Richard, Archbishop of Paris, condemned the work as 'calculated to trouble the faith of Catholics' on certain vital points of doctrine.

As Loisy remarks:

I thought it probable that my declarations (he refers not only to *L'Évangile et l'Église* but also to the subsequent work, *Autour d'un petit livre*) would be thus misunderstood in spite of my most careful efforts to distinguish between the historical and the theological point of view; despite the care I took not to exaggerate this antagonism, and in spite of the suggestions for their provisional conciliation.

And yet I suppose this 'misunderstanding' could have been well foreseen, and was actually more or less foreseen by Loisy himself. Such prevision of a possibility, or even a probability, could not have made his attempt less honest and sincere.

In December of the same year, 1903, a Roman condemnation followed and confirmed that of Cardinal Richard—five works in all were condemned.

On December 29th he wrote to von Hügel: 'I am resolved to receive the condemnation with respect, saving the rights of conscience and my opinions as an historian.'[1]

Elsewhere, in a letter published in *The Times*, April 30th, 1904, he says: 'Catholic I was, Catholic I remain; critic I was, critic I remain.'[2]

On January 11th, 1904, he wrote his reply to the Roman condemnation; a letter addressed to Cardinal Merry del Val. In it he says that he accepts respectfully the decision of the S. Congregation, and condemns all that may be reprehensible in his writings; but declares that he regards the measure as disciplinary. He is aware that his opinions are not scientifically final; that they are liable to correction; but he can only say what he sees, in the measure that he sees it.[3]

Through all this long, sad story the desire of the sufferer to remain in the Church, and to carry on his work on her

---

[1] *Mém.* II, 290.   [2] *Idem*, p. 311.   [3] *Idem*, pp. 313, 314.

behalf, is poignantly evident. But it is equally evident that
he was, throughout, at the disadvantage of being forced to
exercise a certain reticence. He was working for the future
even more than for the present; he knew that those to whom
he had to address himself had no understanding of the problem; but he believed that the Church was greater than any
of her passing representatives. Thus he says of *L'Évangile et
l'Église*: 'it was an apology for the Catholicism that should
be, and a discreet criticism of actual official Catholicism.'[1]

However, inspired by his genuine love for the Church, and
influenced by the many friends who desired to keep him in it,
he wrote to the Pope himself, and made a last tragic effort for
peace:

Holy Father, I know your goodness and appeal to your
heart. I want to live and die in the communion of the Catholic
Church, and I do not want to contribute to the ruin of faith
in my country. I cannot destroy in myself the results of my
work. So far as lies in my power I submit to the judgment
passed on my writings....
As proof of my sincerity, and to pacify minds, I am prepared
to renounce my teaching in Paris, and to suspend the scientific
publications which I have in preparation.[2]

The response was, alas! very different from what he had
hoped for. It was sent through Cardinal Richard, and the
opening words were as follows: 'I have received a letter from
Abbé Loisy...he appeals to my heart; but the letter was not
written from his own heart, etc.'[3]

The sentence was never forgotten; and I well remember
Loisy, in speaking to us at Pontigny and recounting the story,
saying: 'When I heard those words something broke in my
heart'; he never recovered from them; and though he made
one more effort the result was inevitable; he began to feel, as
he noted, that his place was outside the Church.

Dear parents (he wrote in his journal), who sleep in peace
in our village cemetery, I shall perhaps not rest beside you,

[1] *Mém.* II, 321.   [2] *Idem*, p. 351.
[3] *Idem*, p. 360.

but I do not deny you, nor do I renounce your faith. I am with you; you are with me....I know that you help and encourage me, and that you do not blame me.[1]

And then, to his friends, he expressed the desire to be left in peace; peace being the one right that remained to him; and his only other wish in the matter was not to harm those who had compromised themselves for him. On November 1st, 1906, he celebrated his last Mass.

All this happened before the appearance of the *Syllabus Lamentabile* and the Encyclical *Pascendi*, July 3rd, 1907, and September 8th, 1907.

For those not familiar with these documents it is enough to say that they were directed against what was termed, for the first time, Modernism; and the list of errors was chiefly drawn from the works of Loisy, though others were likewise affected, and even Newman himself was not wholly immune. The story has been told in many places, and all that concerns us here is Loisy's own reaction. At the close of his short work, entitled *Simples réflexions sur le Décret et sur l'Encyclique* Pascendi, he says:

The Pope has said truly that he could not keep silence without betraying the deposit of traditional doctrine...the two positions are taken...the divorce is complete....It is impossible to foresee when and how modern thought and society can be reconciled with the Catholic faith and institution....The wrongs are not all on one side....Time is the great master.... We need despair neither of our civilization, nor of the Church. But one cannot usefully speak to them of reconciliation at a time when they are turning their backs on one another.[2]

That last is a pregnant sentence. The story of so-called Modernism is the story of the impact of science on faith, and the resistance of faith to science. Many lives were lost in the great contest—I mean not human lives, but the lives of Catholics and members of the Church. For the most part those men were not rebels; they were not attacking the Church

---

[1] *Mém.* II, 372.
[2] *Simples réflexions sur le Décret et sur l'Encyclique* Pascendi, pp. 288–289.

nor hostile to her, even though bitter words may have passed their lips in the heat of the fray. But the prevailing note in the letters and journals of Loisy is one of sadness:

> I have given myself much trouble for nothing at all. I took my life and the Church seriously, I have lost the latter and troubled the first.[1]

> The crisis of faith, be it good or evil, was not brought about by my publications. I am its victim rather than its agent. Seeing that it was inevitable, I endeavoured to moderate it; and it was perhaps this presumption that wrecked my life. . . .[2]

Had he shut himself up in purely secular science, he might have been 'pointed to as an example of the concord between science and faith, precisely because he had devoted himself to science only and never talked of faith'.

One asks oneself at the end of it all: 'Was the tragedy inevitable?' I think it was. Not all that happened; not the uncharitable bickerings of the *bonne presse*; not the jealousy and intransigence of those who thought that *they* only held the truth; not the hard words of superiors. But the tragedy was inevitable in so far as, in every war, a certain number, and they of the best, must be sacrificed, either because they are fighting in the front line, or because their homes are being devastated behind the lines. And this was a war; a war between the custodians of faith and pioneers or custodians of science. But a war of minds and souls is not the same thing as a war of brute force, for its actions result not so much in conquest as in inter-penetration. Loisy said that there was an ineluctable opposition between the theological and the historical points of view.[3] This is only true of theology in its static, not in its dynamic, form; and it is not true of faith; not true of the Church past as well as present, in her whole development and history.

Actually the Church, in all these recurring intellectual crises of her history, is always in a state of internal as well as external

---

[1] *Mém.* II, 379.   [2] *Idem*, p. 553.
[3] *Idem*, p. 365.

warfare. The struggle is going on within as well as without; she is struggling with her own digestion as well as with hostile outside forces, and of course her own children stir up the process more unpleasantly than any number of avowed enemies. She can better defend herself from the latter, and continue longer in a state of peaceful quiescence; not dealing directly with the pabulum which she has got to absorb in the end. For religion cannot exist apart from the life of mankind; unending resistance to the movement of that life would result in death. And, as we look back on the history of the Church, we know that the resistance always does come to an end, not by surrender to an outside force, but by the incorporation of that force into her own life. But, like every living thing, she must do it in her own way; a way that is often unjust to her victims, who have to suffer because the Church herself is in the throes of digestive pains.

And for this process of digestion time is needed. The body of the Church is vast and complex; the life-giving blood must circulate through the whole system, and even though the action be unconscious every organ of the Church has some part in the process of assimilation.

Perhaps the Church has not always shown sufficient faith in her own spiritual character. This is what Loisy tried to indicate when he repeatedly asserted that the spiritual essence of doctrines was not impugned by history. Perhaps the Church, or, rather, her representatives, have tried to be right in domains not under her sway; have claimed scientific as well as religious infallibility. This is to make enemies of those who are not necessarily hostile. And in so far as she has done this, she has failed to bring all things into the service of God; she has gained temporary appeasement at the cost of true peace. But willy-nilly the process goes on.

No one can live within the Church at present without realizing that 'Modernism' has been absorbed as well as condemned; that it has, in its own measure, brought about a larger spirit; and that much is said which could not have been said had men like Loisy, Tyrrell, von Hügel, not lived and spoken. To end with a passage from Loisy himself:

I showed how the Christian and Catholic religion had been, from the Gospel onwards, a movement of religious life that had had perpetually to assimilate the elements of its existence and growth, by virtue of a principle sufficiently powerful to accomplish such realization.[1]

[1] *Mém.* II, 392.

CHAPTER VI

ISOLATION

HAVING studied, so far, Loisy's mental and religious evolution within the Church, I should like, before going on to the consideration of his treatment of religious themes in general, to examine the meaning and significance of his attitude in regard to the Church when he found himself outside her. That attitude was, on the whole, consistent, to the end of his life, but not so consistent as to exclude some variety of judgments and utterances. But we have here to study his first reaction and its significance, because by that reaction his eventual and final position to the Church can, to a great extent, be estimated.

Years before the final stroke he had prepared a scheme of life. He was going to inhabit a cottage lent him by friends, and he summed up the future thus:

No hope of any future situation.
Moderate work, unhurried . . . to diversify reading.
To take healthy air and exercise, and to take interest in the little home.
To live in joy and peace so far as possible.
Pius X has imperiously ordered me not to try to save the Church.[1]

And elsewhere:

Whatever be the future fate of Catholicism, I can do nothing.
What will be the religion of the future? I know not.
Roman Catholicism, as it is, must perish and deserves no regret. It could survive by transforming itself, but it will not. It is not my business to will for it. Let us seek peace.[2]

Did he suffer much when it was all over? I think it is impossible to answer the question because he could not have answered it himself. None of us know how much we are, or are not, suffering under certain circumstances. He was cer-

[1] *Mém.* ii, 398.   [2] *Idem*, p. 380.

tainly glad to end the long-drawn battle; he was glad to be
free; he was glad to have to face no more interviews with
ecclesiastical superiors; he was glad to be discharged of any
further responsibility regarding those who looked up to him;
he was glad to speak and write and publish exactly what he
thought.

But the aim of his lifetime had been the intellectual regeneration of the Church, and that aim had been frustrated.
And the home of his mind and soul had been the Catholic
Church, from which he was now excluded. Most of his best
friends were Catholics and they remained behind him, in the
place which he was leaving. In his apostrophe to his dead
parents he gave some vent to feelings that, for the most part,
he kept in his own heart. But, for myself, I cannot believe
but that he suffered more than he admitted, and that there
must have been periods of deep desolation, and of a bitter
sense of homelessness, a sense to which he would never have
given direct expression. But indirect—yes, at times. Here are
two examples.

He was present at a meeting at Pontigny which Louis Canet
and I both attended. On the Sunday morning Canet came
and told me that he had found Loisy at the gate of the Abbey,
listening to the chant of the Mass in the Abbey Church—unable
to enter. And Canet remarked 'should he himself go in and
leave him outside—he could not bear to do so'.

Much later we have a noteworthy letter to Paul Desjardins,
who copied the following passage for me—the date being
1934:

Not long ago I followed the closure of the Eucharistic Congress at Buenos Ayres on the radio. I heard, as though I were
present, the Mass chanted by Cardinal Pacelli; I even received
the Pontifical blessing at the end. And I felt as though a
movement of the total life of our planet, of the universal life,
moral and physical, were passing over the electric current.

He told us, in his *Mémoires*, how he rejoiced in the services
and liturgy of the Church in his seminary days. And again,
his friendship with Henri Brémond, and his assiduous reading

of the great mystical work of the latter, is surely another proof
of a love that was never quite extinguished.

But however this may be, the first reaction from the termina-
tion of the crisis was one of happy relief. He tells us, in the
opening page of the third volume of his *Mémoires*, that he was,
actually, fifty-one years old, but that the number of years did
not express his age—he was already old and tired—and if
excommunication had restored his liberty it had left him without hope of action in the world. Still he had a perfect sense
of inward peace, such as he had not known since, as a child,
he helped his mother in the garden.

And so it was a case of separation, definite and entire; he did
not adopt what has been termed the 'doorstep' policy, it was
not in his mental character to do so. Von Hügel would have
had him act differently. He was even distressed by his prompt
abandonment of the *soutane*, whereas Loisy considered that to
keep it would be to act as a rebel; he considered himself as
neither rebellious nor submissive—he was simply an outsider.

Now one Modernist claim, which von Hügel very earnestly
upheld, was that the Church was greater, was even in some
sense other, than her official representatives; hence to be condemned by these was not to be cut off from the spiritual body.
And this was the attitude that von Hügel hoped to see his
friend assume. Even his mistaken wish for him to continue
to wear clerical garb was one symptom of this policy. But, as
I have maintained, Loisy ceased to be a Modernist when he
ceased to be a Catholic priest; and he renounced the hopes of
Modernism when he renounced his work for the Church.

As he writes:

[Von Hügel] will not understand that excommunication
will alter my position; he will not recall all that I have told him
of the interior process of my thought, and of how I realised in
advance that the decision would put me outside the Church.
He had his own programme, his own vision for me—to remain
in the Church even though banished from her—and he will
never forgive me for not conforming to it.[1]

[1] *Mém.* II, 612–613.

In another place he says:

I could not, as he [von Hügel] would have desired, make an ardent protestation of fidelity to the ideal Catholicism that I had defended in my first little books, since the consistency and future of that Catholicism depended on the existing Church, which could have recognized or tolerated that conception, but which totally rejected it. . . . [Von Hügel] was not wrong in saying that, if I abandoned Catholicism, my secession would be misjudged. He was to be the first to misunderstand and condemn it. . . . Many others, having known me as a Modernist, would have liked to compel me to remain, simply to avoid modifying the application of their own theories on my account.[1]

The case of Loisy was one of the many instances that von Hügel encountered—his chess-board thwarted his plans—the pieces were too much alive!

Loisy's mind was a French mind, and a positive mind. Many non-Catholics, who condemn the Modernist attitude of other Catholics, would stoutly defend his view; for, they would say with him, 'how can you claim to belong to the Church when the Church says you do not?' But this is precisely the question which could be answered in more than one way, and Loisy only answered it as he did because he came to think that the whole movement had proved itself unpractical and unsound.

In one of his letters Loisy remarked that he had not the makings of a heretic or heresiarch, and this saying casts light on the question. There are minds, and I know such, that are fundamentally heretical, even though their owners may be true members of the Church and uphold her doctrine. Their heretical character consists in the fact that they never think any doctrine, religious or even scientific, to be so through and through, so unimpeachably true, as to exclude all questioning and doubt. A recent writer has said that he has discovered the fallacy of supposing that a thing must always be either 'this or that', *entweder*, *oder*; for it may be both 'this and that'.[2] This is the mind of the heretic, that will not adhere to any statement so closely and irrevocably as to exclude all possibility of future development and interpretation.

[1] *Mém.* II, 631.   [2] D. R. Davies, *On to Orthodoxy.*

Now in regard to religious doctrine, there is the heresy that denies, but there is also the heresy that refuses complete assent, in the belief that the doctrine, as it stands, is but a partial statement of religious truth, which lies behind and beyond it. This is not heresy in the technical and defined sense; but, though not outspoken, I do consider that it is a form of latent heresy, not inconsistent with whole-hearted adherence to the Church. And I term it *latent* heresy because, if it were to be given outward expression, it would be condemned as heresy. And it is as well that such 'heretics', according to my definition, do not, as a rule, speak out their inner belief, for they might constitute a formidable list.

Loisy's earliest quarrel was with orthodoxy, and though, at first, he deemed that spiritual truth was wider than its orthodox presentment he ended by abandoning this position, and identifying the Church with her official and orthodox rulers. And in maintaining and acting upon this view he was actually maintaining the strictly orthodox position, unlike those who held to the Church despite her officials. And as he thus renounced the Modernist hopes, he also renounced the Church.

Mr Davies is paradoxical, but I may well deserve the same imputation when I describe those Modernists who remained in the Church as, in a sense, more *heretical* than those who, like Loisy, accepted their *quietus*. They were heretics according to the orthodox conception of truth; and this because, for them, truth was wider, deeper and more far-reaching than any of the formulas in which men confined it. Religious doctrine dealt with truths beyond the capacity of human understanding or description; and let us go further and say that, in a lesser degree, so does scientific truth. There are scientific as well as religious heretics; minds that never adhere so completely, even to the established dicta of science, as not to think that the forces of the universe may be ever, in great part, recalcitrant to our theories in their regard; that we measure the universe with human instruments, and that the universe may not be measurable by such. Scientific truth is sound according to our own methods, but those methods are our own. And so I know of scientific as well as religious heretics, who, in both cases, do not repudiate either religious or scientific doctrine, but cherish an element of doubt as to its full final significance. Catholics may object to my definition of heresy, and yet I would ask a certain number—without expecting an answer—whether they would swear to being completely innocent of the form of dogmatic acquiescence which I have described as latent heresy.

And so we find Loisy in a state of definite, and so far as he foresaw, final separation from the Church. But he left her with no hostile intention, and he never turned his guns upon her. I well remember that, on the occasion of his 70 years Jubilee, to which I had been invited, he asked me to suspend my decision until he had assured himself that the meeting would not have an anti-clerical character.

If (he wrote, October 14th, 1926) the Congress threatened to become an anti-religious and anti-Catholic manifestation, I should not hesitate to withdraw from it. I do not expect that I shall be obliged to do this, and I hope that all will go well. But as I am not perfectly certain, it is my duty to warn you. If you think well, you could, in your answer to the Secretary of the Council, announce your subject while adding that you will count on me for its realization.[1]

And in another letter to myself he had spoken of an article of mine in the *Hibbert Journal* which did actually treat of those who followed a contrary policy to his own, and remained faithful to the Church. I had said:

In any religion that speaks to the heart of man there must be some element of Divine Revelation; in the expression of every Divine Revelation there must be some human element. Every Church has to serve out its forms of worship as well as its articles of belief; so long as, in that Church, we find and feel the highest teaching of spiritual reality, we accept her doctrine, her discipline, her objects of worship. . . . God could reveal Himself in other Churches and in other ways—the God of the Christian Church has revealed Himself in that way and no other. If therefore we would worship in that temple, we must worship according to the ways of that temple.[2]

[1] Letter is subjoined.
[2] *Hibbert Journal*, April 1922, p. 209.

In regard to these words Loisy wrote (April 16th, 1922):
'As what the world needs is an *existing* religion, your personal
position is sound and dependable.'

It was an attitude he could not share, but this lack of
hostility to the Church from which he had been ousted, and
which he had then voluntarily renounced, is somewhat rare in
such cases, and is distinctly significant. It was not with religion
that his quarrel consisted; it was not with the Church as a
purely religious organ. He was religious as a Catholic, and
he never ceased to be religious. His ulterior development, and
his fundamental spiritual faith, have yet to be studied.

On the Congrès d'histoire du Christianisme for his own
Jubilee

Ceffonds, October 14th, 1926.

. . . . . .

I answer your kind letter, beginning from the end.

They have asked you for a communication at the Congress
which will be held in Paris in April 1927, and you propose as
your subject *Tyrrell—von Hügel*, that is to say an essay on
Catholic Modernism in England. They were right to ask you
and I can only approve your choice of subject. But I must
give you some particulars in regard to this Congress. From
the beginning I warned the organizers that they must not
make a tendentious manifestation of it. I should have preferred
that B—— were not on the committee. I have no objection
to your choice of article, because I think I know you well
enough, and know that you will treat it historically. The project
has been menaced, and still is, from two sides—from the right
a dumb opposition; ... on the left a certain confusion arose
because I had associated Jean Baruzi as my *suppléant* in the
Collège de France for the coming year, as though I had thus
compromised the majesty of pure science and made a retrograde
motion towards the Church. The excitement has subsided,

. . . . . .

PART II

CHAPTER VII

CHRIST & CHRISTIANITY

THE critical studies of his early days, and Scripture exegesis, continued to be Loisy's main occupation to the end of his life. But when I say 'main occupation' it is not to exclude a persistent pre-occupation with definitely religious subjects. I should enumerate, in this later period, no fewer than nine or ten small volumes (one might include even a larger number) consecrated to purely religious and moral considerations. It is with the message of those later works that this second part of my study will deal; and it is, indeed, largely the sense of their importance that inspires the whole of this attempt. But before commencing this later analysis I do not want to by-pass a subject which held a main position in his critical as in his more exclusively religious works; a subject that belongs to both periods of his life, and that therefore constitutes a bridge between the two: the subject, namely, of Christ, of the Gospel, of Christianity. And for the study of this subject one may refer to early and to later works, throughout which we may find differences of feeling and character, but no real opposition of statement in the critical order.

In the volume entitled *Autour d'un petit livre*, the 'petit livre' being the much noted, much lauded, much execrated work entitled *L'Évangile et l'Église*, we have, I think, one of the fullest expositions of his treatment of the Christological problem. This work consists of a series of letters on different points, and the one to which I would now refer is that addressed to Archbishop Mignot on the 'Divinity of Jesus Christ'. It would be impossible to find a single point of her teaching on which the Church would be more acutely sensitive than that of the dogma of the Divinity of Christ, and this was one of the main points—not the only one—on which the apologetic volume *L'Évangile et l'Église* was condemned.

Those of us who might most wish to do so would be shirking the truth if we denied that, in Loisy's later works, there was, at times, a hardness in his treatment of this doctrine, a predominance of the critical over the religious outlook, which did not qualify his earlier works. He was no longer a Catholic believer; his early faith was dead; he was looking elsewhere than to the Church for the spiritual future of mankind. But in his apologetic work of the earlier period his aim was to show that, while history must not be denied, neither should the essential doctrines of the Church suffer eclipse. And he believed that he had found the way of reconciliation through what we may almost call a discovery, because it was the perception of a truth (I will dare to call it a truth) that had not been recognized by theologians or critics, whether Christian or hostile. And this discovery was a reversal of the traditional belief that the teaching of the Church was grounded on, proved and supported by the Scriptures, whereas, in fact, the New Testament Scriptures had their origin within and not without the Church; the Church did not depend on them for her truth and her life, but they on her. They were the utterance of her early faith, and were carried with her, along the ages, in her process of adaptation to the spiritual needs of mankind.

And while, as I have said, we may find in Loisy's writings, of what I will specially call his middle period, a hardening in regard to the Christological as well as other Christian dogmas, on this point he did not vary to the last, for the simple reason that, when he ceased to treat it from the apologetic standpoint, he continued to maintain all sound historical positions. I believe that Loisy sometimes divined that his work might prove, in the far future, more valuable for the cause of faith than living Christian apologists now dare imagine.

If I speak for myself I am sure that I speak for many others when I admit that history has caused us many a heartache, in its disturbance of the peaceful assumptions of faith; along with the Church, we have had to digest new and unaccustomed food. But history has been a saving as well as a destroying factor, and in defending the rights of history Loisy, both early and late, defended the rights of faith. And though he steadfastly denied (whether rightly or wrongly) that history could prove, even from the words of Christ, the doctrine of His Divinity, he also saved Christ from what I should term *manipulation*, on the part of Christians, whether learned, or well-meaning, who have either endeavoured to find in Him the protagonist of their own religious faith, or the precursor of their own political party, or the pleasant 'man of the world', with, as I lately heard a preacher describe Him, an habitual 'twinkle in the eye'.

And still more emphatically did he defend the historic reality of the person of Jesus Christ from its obliteration by those who would have left Christianity standing without Christ. His very latest works were consecrated to the refutation of this theory.

In *L'Évangile et l'Église*, which was directed, chiefly, against the theory put forward by Adolf Harnack in his *Wesen des Christentums*, which confined the message of Christ to that of the Fatherhood of God, he says:

Harnack tried to conciliate Christian faith with the demands of science and the scientific spirit of our time. These demands must have been, or have seemed to be, very great, for faith is reduced to small and modest proportions. What would Luther have thought? . . . If religion is thus brought into accord with science, it is because they no longer meet.[1]

In *Autour d'un petit livre* he quotes, in the letter to which I have already referred, the text of Acts ii, 36: 'Therefore let all the house of Israel know assuredly, that God hath made that same Jesus, whom ye have crucified, both Lord and Christ'; and he maintains that 'this simple distinction, made

---

[1] *L'Évangile et l'Église*, p. xii.

from the beginning by Peter and Paul, but often neglected ever since, is the foundation of *L'Évangile et l'Église*'.[1]

Further on he says:

Jesus Himself lived on earth in the consciousness of His Humanity, and He spoke in accordance with that consciousness; He lived in the consciousness of His Messianic vocation, and He taught according to His consciousness of that vocation. . . . The Divinity of Christ is a dogma that has grown in the Christian conscience, but that was not expressly formulated in the Gospel; it existed only in germ in the notion of the Messias, Son of God.[2]

He describes, later:

the continual effort of faith to comprehend more perfectly an object that is beyond it. The effort is made by steps, and the final term is not reached at once; one may even say that it is not yet reached. . . . Every stage of faith is like a trial and an obstacle, to be surmounted by the divine force of its inner principle.[3]

Further on:

The historic Christ, in the humility of His "service", is great enough to justify Christology, and Christology does not need, for its truth, to have been expressly taught by Jesus.[4]

Again:

There are only two sane attitudes for the interpretation of the Gospel, that of the historian, who takes it as it is, and endeavours to analyse the character and original meaning of the texts, and that of the Church, which, without regard to the limitations of its primitive sense, draws from the Gospel the teaching that is suitable to the needs of modern times.[5]

Again:

The Christological doctrine is a transcendent explanation of the historic fact.[6]

And in the *Livre Inédit*, to which we have already referred, he writes:

The Resurrection of Jesus was not the last step of His terrestrial career, the last act of His ministry amongst men, but

---

[1] *Autour d'un petit livre*, pp. 111–112.   [2] *Idem*, pp. 116–117.
[3] *Idem*, pp. 119–120.   [4] *Idem*, p. 136.
[5] *Idem*, p. 143.   [6] *Idem*, pp. 147–148.

the first article of the faith of the Apostles and the spiritual foundation of Christianity.[1]

And in a striking passage of *Autour d'un petit livre* he indites those who would draw Christ into the circle of contemporary life:

People who profess to show the perfect harmony of the Gospel with the necessities of present life, with social equity, political order and progress, may have been scandalized by finding in my book [*L'Évangile et l'Église*] that Jesus was simply indifferent to all these temporal objects. It is a fact. Had I found in the Gospel a programme of civilization, or an ideal of Christian democracy, I would have made a point of informing my readers.[2]

Time rolled on; Loisy abandoned all his early aims at Christian apology, but, by a strange fate, or by a mysterious disposition of Providence, he actually became, in the last years of his life, an apologist in a new sense, a defender of the historic actuality of Christ. We have *Le Mandéisme* in 1934, which deals with the substitution of John the Baptist for Jesus Christ as the origin of Christianity. But, above all, we have his *Histoire et Mythe à propos de Jésus Christ*, which is his answer to the *Mystère de Jésus* of Paul Couchoud, and his *Jésus le Dieu fait homme*, of which the English translation was to be entitled *The Creation of Christ*. This author's idea was that the belief in Christ as God preceded, did not follow, the history of the life of Jesus Christ on earth; that, in fact, Christianity was not founded on the historic Christ, but created His history. 'Let us leave the man and keep the god. Historians, do not hesitate to efface the man Jesus from your pages.'

Now Loisy was ever more roused to opposition by anything in the nature of a quasi-scientific myth than by the most extravagant myths that were inspired by religious faith. In this case he denounced the theory of M. Couchoud as totally unscientific. He wrote in *La Naissance du Christianisme*:

Whatever may be said in the opposite sense, there is not a Christian document of the first ages that does not imply

[1] *Mém.* 1, 454.   [2] *Autour d'un petit livre*, p. 145.

the historicity of Jesus; for even heretic Gnostics, who denied
the materiality of the Body of Christ, and the physical reality
of His passion, believed, with the mass of Christians, in the
historicity of Jesus and of His earthly manifestation; their
Christ, at once visible and immaterial, was not for them a
phantom without reality, a being of pure vision, as some
mythologists[1] would make Him. And pagan authors, the least
favourable to Christianity, from Tacitus to Celsus and the
emperor Julian, regarded Jesus as an historical personage.[2]

He goes on to say in what way he conceives of myth in
regard to Christ; on that point we will speak further on. He
certainly had not the faith of the Church, but he firmly
believed in the true existence and life of the Man who walked
on earth. The mystical faith in Christ was not a product of
the religious life of the early community, it was bound up with
the historical fact of the life of Jesus Christ.[3] And, with a burst
of exasperation, he writes:

Let us end this folly. For Paul, Jesus was a son of Israel,
who died on the Cross and was raised up by God, Who consti-
tuted Him 'Christ' and 'Lord'.[4]

In the earlier work, *La Naissance du Christianisme*, we have
a like protest against what he regards as unhistoric attempts
to base Christianity on an air-borne foundation. With, I
suspect, that smile for which he had, in his younger days, been
reproached, he writes: 'the author of this book humbly acknow-
ledges that he has failed to discover that Jesus did not exist'.

He then goes on to say:

The somewhat noisy conjectures of some people, who have
sought to explain Christianity without the one whom Christianity regards as its Founder, seem to me somewhat fragile.
These conjectures arise generally from persons who have
arrived late at the problem of Jesus, and who have not pre-
viously made any profound study of the history of Israel and
of Christianity. The non-existence of Jesus is, for them, an

[1] Referring to M. Couchoud in particular.
[2] *La Naissance du Christianisme*, pp. 82–83.
[3] See *Histoire et Mythe à propos de Jésus Christ*, p. 240.
[4] *Idem*, p. 244.

element of a philosophical system, unless their intention be avowedly or tacitly polemical. For Dupuis, Christ was a solar myth; for Bruno Bauer and the Dutch school—except van Manen—he was simply the creation of Alexandrian allegorism; as also according to Smith, Drews, Robinson. With us P. L. Couchoud and E. Dujardin have followed particular paths, Couchoud postulating a pre-Christian myth of the suffering Jahve, which a vision of Simon Peter suddenly transformed into a living religion; Dujardin a pre-Christian cult of Jesus, with the fictitious crucifixion of an individual playing the part of God, etc.[1]

In the later work, of 1938, he writes that he was moved 'by the grave circumstances of the day' to intervene. He says, pathetically:

I know, by long experience, that my voice does not carry far, and I realise that it is now failing. But I know also and I feel deeply that, in the midst of this world chaos, the question of Christian origins is passing through a very grave crisis which may be of great consequence.[2]

And further on:

Contrary to what Couchoud has said, these things did not take place outside time or in the heights of the firmament. . . . Before the commentaries of that mystical faith, whose connection with the historic fact of Jesus has been misunderstood by Couchoud, there was the fact itself, and it was from the fact of the Crucified Jesus that primitive faith proclaimed his resuscitation as Christ and Lord with God.[3]

But this was not Loisy's last pronouncement on myth-making from preconceived theories.

Later in the same year he produced yet another volume;[4] which he sent me inscribed 'ultime souvenir', though actually there was one more.

In his 'avant-propos' he writes:

I humbly acknowledge that my senile activity (*sic*) was so absorbed in Couchoud that I completely forgot Dujardin,

---

[1] *La Naissance du Christianisme*, p. 6.
[2] *Histoire et Mythe à propos de Jésus Christ*, p. 11.
[3] *Idem*, p. 240.
[4] *Autres Mythes à propos de la Religion*.

whose myth, at once less violent and more prolix than that of Couchoud, merits equal consideration.

It would also have been difficult to discuss them both together, for although they claim to be allied they are distinctly different, Couchoud's central point being the metamorphosis into history, through the initiative of Marcion, of a myth that sprang from Jewish apocalyptic; while the essential thesis of Dujardin is the sudden eruption, in the year 27 of our era, of a prehistoric cult of an immolated, dying and resuscitated god, which cult was transformed by a single stroke, first into a discreet, but later into a bold propaganda of a mystery of salvation, adapted to the profound social needs of the Greco-Roman world.[1]

For a man who had spent his life in the serious examination of documents, and for whom the history of Christian origins was one of the most vital histories of mankind, these attempts to substitute the work of pure imagination for the work of research; to begin at a self-chosen point instead of at the remote, even though dimly perceptible beginning; to spring over the process and establish a position independent of all true relation to the past; were nothing short of exasperating. From the scientific point of view he would gladly have regarded such attempts as negligible, but unfortunately the mental sloth and ignorance of ordinary men and women are such that a cheap theory is easily accepted. Thus it happened that, some years earlier, in 1934, he produced a volume to demonstrate the ineptitude of new theories in regard to the sect of Mandeism. 'Systematic and absolute suppositions', he writes, 'are out of place in the complex and fluid question of Christian origins.'[2]

In pursuing this study I have often wished that Loisy had given us a definition of the word myth, or an explanation of the sense in which he employs it. For it certainly seems to me that, in his denunciation of a certain myth-making process, from which he suffered in his own person,[3] as well as in his conception of history, he is dealing with a different form of

[1] *Idem*, p. 5.
[2] *Le Mandéisme et les Origines Chrétiennes*, p. 156 (1935).
[3] See *Un mythe apologétique*, 1939.

myth from that which sprang, in his judgment, from the process and evolution of Christian history and Christian faith.

These later myths, whether they convinced their own makers or not, were made and turned out as it were in one piece; they were fabricated out of hand; and if they had any chance of proving themselves not mere myths it would only be by finding their source far behind any of the facts that were actually adduced as their origin.

For these myths Loisy had no patience; they seemed to him a deliberate attempt to insert foreign matter into the tissue of history.

What then about Christian myths, and his treatment of them?

Not the most earnestly believing Catholic would deny that the artificial and fabricated myth has played its part in the history of the faith, as elsewhere. We come daily across pious inventions, bogus prophecies and miracles, that catch on to the minds of the credulous, and run their course, until they wither from want of spiritual sustenance. But there is also a mythical process which is an element of the religious process itself; which is no mere invention, no artificial product, but the mode of expression of faith when it reaches out from the known to the unknown, from the facts of history to their spiritual significance. And it is here that we need, for the understanding of every religion, even the most spiritual, some knowledge of the earliest utterings of human religion. The theologian is apt to shy from the word *magic*, and yet is there not truth in the words of Loisy in his *Essai sur le Sacrifice* that:

The avowed proofs of mystical faith, though more elaborated in the higher religions, are not better established in principle or confirmed in experience than those of the magic of uncivilized men? [1]

Are we not learning daily more and more that the exclusiveness of creeds conduces to weakness, and not strength, and that we can none of us afford to deny our debt to our forebears?

[1] *Essai sur le Sacrifice*, p. 526.

Christianity can much more fearlessly acknowledge its relationship to the early religions of magic, with their mythical parables, than she can accept any connection with the later 'myths' that Loisy denounced; and this because the latter are fictions of artifice, whereas the former are the spontaneous creations of faith; superstitious and ignorant, but full of human, even spiritual, meaning.

A very noteworthy sign in much contemporary religious thinking, of the bolder and more original character, is its fearless treatment of what Loisy—like others—has termed religious myth. The purely rationalistic attitude seems to be outgrown; there is a more living recognition of life, in whatever form life may express itself; and in so far as religious faith expresses itself in myth, such myth is no longer regarded as mere fiction and fairy tale, but as a development of the religious consciousness.

Now Loisy was a critic and an historian, and, for him, a true historic fact was a true historic fact, and a myth was not an historic fact. And yet the very contrast—though not avowedly stated because he had no occasion to do so—between his treatment of theories such as those of Couchoud and Dujardin, and his treatment of what he would term the Christian myth is significant. And surely the difference is this— that in the former case there was an attempt to *substitute* a myth for history, whereas in the religious process the myth becomes the spiritual clothing and expression of historic fact; and the history becomes at last subsumed into the whole body of faith.

And here again we come on that opinion of Loisy, which was, for him, a definite conviction and not a mere opinion, that the Scriptures were, in the life of the Church, doctrinal in character rather than historical.

Thus, in a very important letter to von Hügel of May 22nd, 1894, he writes:

It does not seem that the Bible is *sufficiently inspired*, or could have been, to be regarded, in itself alone, as the true master in religion. It is only its *witness*.[1]

[1] *Mém.* 1, 332 (Loisy's italics).

And further:

Theology has her formulas, which she guards and interprets. We must take them in her own sense. . . . The truth of Scripture is to be understood according to the general intention of Providence, and the particular purpose of each book. . . there are many things in Scripture which are not true, and which could not have been true without upsetting the very notion of the book or the metaphysical conditions of human intelligence. . . or without upsetting moral conditions, such as an historical exactitude which our moderns seek but fail to attain.[1]

From the *Livre Inédit* we may draw a still more pertinent quotation:

For the first Christian generation, and particularly for St Paul, the Resurrection of Christ was not the miracle in the material order on which later apologetic has so much insisted, it was the Messianic consecration of the lost Master and his glorious immortality. . . . The fact of the resurrection, properly understood, does not belong to the historic and human order.[2]

And in *La Naissance du Christianisme*, referring to the later artificial theories of Christian origins, he says:

In attempting to turn Jesus into a myth critics would embark on a road without an outlet, and on endless subtleties. And yet it is true that Jesus has lived in a myth, and that a myth has borne him to the summit of history.[3]

And, in the same work:

It was on the broken pieces of hope, on the death of Jesus, which should have destroyed their faith, that this same faith of the disciples founded the religion of Jesus the Christ. Only those will be amazed at such a miracle of faith who know not in what religious faith consists, and what it can realize in an enthusiastic and ardent group. Faith unconsciously procures for herself all the illusions necessary to her preservation and progress; and, in so doing, does not always accomplish, from the human point of view, an illusory result.[4]

[1] *Idem.*
[3] *La Naissance du Christianisme*, p. 83.
[2] *Mém.* I, 454.
[4] *Idem*, p. 123.

And now to resume in general Loisy's treatment of religious myth I submit the following conclusions, which are the result of my own reflections, and do not claim to possess documentary authority from his own words.

1. He distinguished firmly between history and myth, and, in fact, a great part of his work is concerned with that very distinction.

2. He distinguished the artificial and self-made myth from the myth that grew spontaneously out of collective belief and faith.

3. He traced this myth-making process throughout religion, and religions, from their earliest human manifestations, so that it seemed to be inseparable from the process of human faith itself, and, indeed, of life itself.

4. He did not, in regard to Christian myth, raise the question of its truth or the reverse; historically it was not founded; it was for faith itself to preserve or reject it.

5. According to his theory that the Scriptures themselves were not, in the main, historical, although based on and containing history, they justifiably included myth as well as historic facts, since both were of the stuff of religious faith, and truth, and doctrine.

6. The value of the myth was in its moral origin and its moral bearing.

I do not know that Loisy ever came into touch with a later school of apologetic and its bolder acceptance of religious myth. We have moved further from the rationalistic conception of truth than Loisy did, or, perhaps, had time to do. Every day one comes on some new and daring pronouncements in this order of thought. Loisy might have been startled by such pronouncements—or perhaps he would not—but in either case I think his philosophy of religious myth is not without significance in regard to this later thought.

For myself I carefully avoid, throughout this work, any assertions in regard to the purely exegetical works. There are positions that may stand, and others that may fall. The negative criticisms may have been, in parts, excessive; there are, to my lay mind, occasional outbreaks of prejudice. But my effort throughout is to find, in spite of all that may shock or displease Catholic feeling, the religious import of Loisy's work and message, and here, on this the cardinal article of our faith, I maintain that he has been the unflinching defender of the reality of that life on earth which is, to the Christian believer, the centre of his religion. He could not find in history any *proof* of the faith that founded itself on the reality of that life; any *proof* for the miracles and manifestations that surrounded its history. But he found in history the source of the faith that is Christianity.

We have had perhaps too much of the facile talk of Christianity without Christ; and, as I study anew this great Christological question, in the life and works of my subject, I come to see that the main task of the Church has been to preserve the faith in Christ and not merely the faith in Christianity; and to preserve faith in Him, not as of one who can suffer adaptation according to the individual mind, or the passing needs of society, but as of one removed beyond the power of human manipulation. That He walked on earth, this is the fact that history will never deny; that He lives in Heaven is the faith which the Church exists to preserve, and, in its measure, to develop. Men are too well disposed to shape Christianity according to their ends, but so long as Christ Himself is real they cannot do with Him what they would do with the mere phantom of a belief and system.

To end with two quotations:

Taken as a whole, the Gospels present a prophetic legend and a liturgy...it is the part of the critic to find what lies behind that liturgy, to discern the facts which conditioned the visions of faith and which are implicit in it...the worst thing that could happen to him would be for him to form a vision which he might think to substitute for those indispensable facts and so offer merely a fantastic interpretation of traditional documents.[1]

[1] *Mém.* III, 442.

Lastly, in his discourse pronounced at the Collège de France, December 5th, 1931, he defends the historians

of the truth of Christianity from the accusation of desiring to dig its grave. We seek rather to be the precursors of its renovation. For what counts and lasts in religion is not its external forms, which are necessarily and continually variable, but the spirit which gives life to the forms, that sense of the divine which guides humanity throughout its moral striving and labour.

CHAPTER VIII

THEOLOGY & SCIENCE

HAD LOISY, in abandoning his ecclesiastical career, abandoned all interest in religion, and devoted himself exclusively to scientific and historical work, there would have been no purpose in the present study. But, actually, the religious interest remained paramount, and not only did religious documents remain the one object of his scientific labour, but religion itself became, almost increasingly, his chief mental preoccupation. One after another he poured forth those shorter works, which, to his abiding resentment, his friend von Hügel treated as negligible, but which were actually, in his opinion, as he once told me, the result of deeper mind and heart searching than what we may call his professional output. Those same studies, which had rendered it impossible for him to retain his original orthodox belief, made it likewise impossible for him—even had he wished, which he did not—to ignore the great and persistent human fact of human faith and religion.

We shall see him crossing swords with those who proposed new myths in the place of Christian myths; he denounced them in the name of history. And in his later works we shall find him opposing the false claims of science as he had opposed the false claims of theology. Theology had come out from her own domain to invade the realm of science, but science, in her turn, was only too readily disposed to squat on land that did not rightly belong to her.

And this is why I persistently believe that, even for those who would never accompany him on the more negative steps of his process, even for those to whom orthodox faith remains firm and respectable, there is something of deep significance in his religious message to mankind.

I regard the earlier part of Loisy's life as vitally important for the understanding of his later evolution, negative or positive. This is why I devoted a chapter to his breach with the orthodox theological presentment of religious truth. That breach was the result of both rational and spiritual dissent from traditional theology. His dissent was rational, in so far as science and history were concerned; it was spiritual in so far as the absolute character of theological doctrine seemed to him incompatible with the mysterious character of religious truth, whose object was impossible of human definition. Like Socrates he held that the wise man was wise just because he did not think he knew what he did not know. Had his labours been accepted, and had he continued his work in the Church, this was precisely the point on which his apologetic efforts would have been founded.

Thus, as early as 1896–1897 in his *Livre Inédit*, he writes:

The world has two faces, one that is visible, phenomenal, material and directly observable, which is the domain of science; the other invisible, interior, spiritual, felt rather than perceived, sought rather than observed, which is the domain of faith. The object seems common to both, but it is not, for, though it may be at bottom the same for both faith and science, they regard it from different angles.

So that the doctrine of faith has nothing to teach science; though it may have much to teach scientists by the influence it can exercise on the moral discipline of their research.[1]

. . . . .

We learn much when we learn our limitations. Religion, revelation, true theology—by which we mean theology which is based on psychology and history—bring to secular knowledge, to the rational and external knowledge of the universe, a precious contribution of experience of another order; giving to scientific knowledge a clearer consciousness of its true frontiers, giving it a moral significance, preserving its eternal significance, setting before it the divine and ideal face of reality, its mysterious and interior life, the religious and transcendent sense of things.

But science renders a corresponding service to theology, which needs, in its turn, to recognize its own limits. It has no right to define the external order of the world and the facts of history, since that external order and those facts are what

[1] *Mém.* I, 471.

they are, independently of all reasoning.... Theology is the
philosophy of revelation; not revelation itself, nor religion; not
faith, nor even, strictly speaking, the object of faith.... Its whole
value is as an interpretation of faith.[1]

'Those facts are what they are'; this is the positive presentment of life; that positivist presentment that, having once
come into its own, as it did very fully in the latter part of the
last century, proceeded to claim more than its own. For not
only were plain material facts to be recognized for what they
were, for plain and undeniable material facts, but nothing else
was to be recognized as real, and if the clever anatomist,
having dissected the human body to its last detail, declared
triumphantly that he had not found the least vestige of a soul,
then no soul could possibly exist.

This is a temper of mind with which we Victorians were very
familiar. I remember raging against it in my youth, when
I was more sure of everything than I now am. But one might
as well, in those days, have butted one's head against a stone
wall; it was the scientific temper of the age.

There are some representatives of that school left, though
a contrary spirit has entered the scientific world. Yet science
still retains much of its exclusive character, and Loisy had not
broken through the barriers of a narrow and exclusivistic
theological school to shut himself up in its scientific counterpart.

He continues in the same place from which we are quoting:

No fact is purely natural or purely supernatural, everything
that happens in the world is both; natural, because it enters
into the series of phenomena, into the factual process, and
supernatural, because the cause of the world and of all that
passes in it can only be apprehended by faith.

These pages are from his *Livre Inédit*, and he adds an amend-
ment:

It should have been said that the transcendent principle
and the supreme value of moral life are the proper objects of
faith, whether this principle be identical or not with that of

[1] *Mém.* I, 472.

the visible universe, which, in its turn, escapes final scientific investigation.[1]

When we pass to his later works and, in particular, to an important one of 1917, *La Religion*, we find, in spite of much that is of a more negative character, the same line of thought. And here again, though speaking under correction, I cannot help noting a kind of analogy between Loisy's religious philosophy and certain recent schools, which boldly pass over and beyond the reach of scientific proof to a spiritual apprehension that is independent of purely rational support. But where Loisy would have dissented from any such efforts would be in so far as they did more than outstrip scientific truth, and actually ran counter to it.

La Religion could not have been written by one who had never doubted any more than by one who had not known an earlier period of unquestioning faith. His quarrel with rationalistic theology, as with rationalistic science, was that both ignored or deformed faith. For in his Catholic days, as in his later ones, he was ever conscious of a certain ineradicable element of human life, of a faith in something beyond the perception of the senses, beyond the scope of reason; of faith in something which defied clear knowledge, and was yet not all unknown. And faith could outlive much perversion and illusion, but it could not outlive the cold touch of rationalism.

From the point of view of strict reasoning, and the relation of what is hoped to what is realized, faith has always comprised a considerable element of illusion. But do not imagine that faith is all illusion. That might be said if faith were identified with the beliefs in which it has been expressed, and which inevitably become outworn. Faith is not belief. . .its deepest principle can no more be defined than its ultimate object. . . . This is why faith outlives, under new forms of religion, the religions that are dead. . . .

This force of faith is the mystery of humanity, and is the point at which this mystery meets and mingles with the mystery of the universe. For in affirming the moral value of human existence faith also affirms, though contrary to all appearance,

[1] *Idem*, p. 472.

the moral significance of the world and of the life that is in the world. If reason discovers the mechanism of the external world, faith perceives intuitively and reveals an inner world which is not mechanism...a world which, in spite of the opposing weight of universal mechanism, escapes and even surmounts it.[1]

And it surmounts it, not by the overcoming of reason, but by not even reasoning.

'The religions known to history were based on affirmation and not on demonstration';[2] this in their origin and early development.

Then came science, first to question, and then to deny, and religion set to work to furnish philosophical proof of her affirmations.

Thus faith called reason to her defence, and a better informed reason constructed more learned defences than those of the ancient apologies; but faith continued to place limits to reason, or, rather, to force it to work on the undisputed postulates of belief.[3]

But

If there be a fact attested by history, it is that the simple explanation which religions have endeavoured to furnish of the world and of life have never resisted examination. Confronted with deeper and clearer knowledge such explanations have appeared mythical, something, that is to say, which is literally untrue, but is like a figurative image of the clearer perception ultimately obtained; it is, in fact, the symbol, solid only in appearance, of the vague reality it attempts to present.

But let not science deem herself totally exempt from all mythical tendency; she passes through many phases of myth in her progress to fuller truth; nor is she ever wholly free from the myth-making process.

Even the general explanations that are now put forward in the name of science contain a considerable element of myth, or are even a more profound form of myth, from which the mysticism has been stripped.[4]

[1] *La Religion*, pp. 183 ff.
[2] *Idem*, p. 70.
[3] *Idem*, p. 71.
[4] *Idem*, pp. 74, 75.

He places the dogmatic theologian and the materialistic scientist side by side for both, in their own way, are rationalizing that which evades reason. The theologian brings reason to bear on faith, he attempts in a measure to bring the unknowable into the region of the known. The scientist forgets that, for him too, there is an unknowable, and denies what cannot be clearly known; he claims to draw mystery from its hiding place, and reduce it to scientific proportions.

Until now (he writes) most of those who, on the grounds of reason and of their personal science, have entered on the examination of religions, have been inclined to regard them simply as childish explanations of the universe, associated with foolish superstitions and customs often as absurd as the beliefs. . . . Since religions failed to furnish a learned explanation of the universe, they cast them aside with ridicule, or devitalized them.

But:

Religion is not an affair of pure reason, to be fashioned by the reasoning of the scholar. The wisest, be he only a man of science, . . . can never draw from his brain a thought capable of acting on the faith of a people for its life and greatness. The mass of men are only moved by what comes from themselves, by a simple, sentient, living idea that a prophet, that is to say one who is the soul of the people and anticipates their aspirations, translates into a language that they can understand.

Nothing is easier to explain than the failure of what the philosophers of the last centuries called natural religion; a cold deism, which was supposed to furnish the last word on the universe, and to provide the basis of duty. Actually it was the Christian faith, stripped of its mystery, the Gospel without Christ, and morality without the Church. It was just a doctrine, not a living faith; a dead hope. . . based on mere reasoning; a rule that the individual was to impose upon himself by reflection and deduction, instead of feeling it as a living force surrounding him and demanding his moral adherence.[1]

. . . .

[1] *La Religion*, pp. 78, 80–81.

Faith is not communicated from reason to reason but from faith to faith, from the believing group to the believing individual . . . it spreads like a spiritual contagion.

As to Deism:

If it fell of itself, in spite of the talent of its advocates and the vogue which some of them enjoyed, it was just because it was itself a contradiction; it was a reasoning that claimed to be faith, a learned opinion that claimed to be a religion. . . . The ancient faith that it thought boastfully to replace actually supplanted it by surviving it; and the discomfiture of this enemy, in whom she might have recognized the abortion of her own theology, brought about a revival of her remaining vitality.[1]

Theology failed in so far as she claimed to be science, science failed in its attempt to take the place of theology. And faith survived both.

This was the truth that Loisy persistently recognized throughout all that seemed to be works of pure demolition. This is why he could read, with passionate interest, such works as those of his friend Henri Brémond, with their patient and subtle analysis of the ardent faith of countless mystics. And this is why he could write to me, in regard to an article of mine, in which I set forth certain definite reasons for fidelity to one's faith, that letter from which I have already quoted. For though, to his mind, Christianity would have to yield its place for another form of religion yet, since this new form had not yet appeared above the horizon, he recognized the value of that which did exist.

This was not mere pragmatism. He had no sympathy with those who would preserve religion 'for the sake of the masses'; for its hygienic properties. If he accepted such a position as I set forth in the article to which his letter referred, it was not from motives of expediency, but because faith, which responded to spiritual reality that lay behind and beyond the direct perceptions of workaday life, could express itself in many and varying ways, and must express itself in some way:

Faith, which is said to work miracles, does in fact work one, one only, but a great one, almost infinite, and infinitely

[1] *La Religion*, p. 82.

beneficial: she holds man erect and confident over the dark abyss over which his existence floats.[1]

The following letter to myself gives further elucidation of the theme of *La Religion*:

Paris, September 29th, 1917.

. . . My book attracts the attention of a small number, I had not counted on many readers. Louis Canet may have told you that I suppressed, in order not to pose as a prophet, some lines at the end of my preface in which I stated that I did not count on the votes of my contemporaries, and left my book, in so far as it possessed any value, to the judgment of the future.

Certainly I believe in the transcendent, in the ideal and its reality, as something other in itself than humanity. But I abstain from defining this otherness, and I have endeavoured to construct my moral religion without metaphysics, without an explicit doctrine of that transcendence that escapes us, though we do not escape it. It seems to me that the economy of faith, which I have endeavoured to sketch, is not for that reason more inadequate than that of religions provided with a metaphysic that is, at bottom, conjectural and outworn. I think that I have preserved the moral significance of the transcendent in relation to humanity. Can the sentiment or intuition of this signification not be acquired without a definition of the unknowable? I think so.

I have given its place to mystical experience. My notion of faith—which struck Bergson—will appear to scientists the height of mysticism. I know some who are furious with it. Here again I think that I am in agreement with the great mystics as regards the moral sense of life and its higher principle. As to particular mystical doctrines I reserve my opinion. They are more or less special and relative as conditioned by time and environment. I think the great mystics would be, in a certain way, the most indulgent critics of my essay, and I have already written to Brémond that our father Fénelon would not have cursed me. He would only have thought that I had perused the *Maximes des Saints* less than *Télémaque*.

[1] *Mors et Vita*, p. 76.

CHAPTER IX

THE IMMANENT & THE TRANSCENDENT

It was on these two words that the long friendship of von Hügel and Loisy foundered; and if I pursue the analysis of this process of alienation it is not for its personal significance, but because it illustrates Loisy's own spiritual philosophy.

To him it seemed that von Hügel's preoccupation on this point amounted to a kind of obsession, and in so far as this conviction was justified it was impossible for the two friends to arrive either at agreement or at any definite statement of disagreement, which may be as consistent with understanding friendship as the former.

We know that von Hügel, after the condemnation of Modernism, retired from the battle behind a new line of defence. He thought that the cause was lost, though it had certainly not been lost to the degree that he imagined. But as his sole effort and one hope had been to carry on a work of enlightenment *within* the Church, and as he saw some of his co-fighters abandon such an effort as hopeless, while others fought on only like a suicide company after a lost battle, while the Church regarded their efforts with indifference, it was not surprising that he decided, in his own case, to remain in the Church and to adopt a more prudent policy. But this was not all. That reactionary policy was not merely in the interests of ecclesiastical safety, for he had likewise become possessed by the fear that many of his former co-workers had fallen into a false Immanentism; an immanentism that tended to the de-personalization of God, and to a lessening of His reality.

Loisy, as we have seen, regarded this prepossession as an almost pathological symptom, but if he was right as regards its nervous manifestations he was not right as regards its fundamental character. It was a consequence of his nervous and excitable constitution that the Baron often perceived the

Bogey where it did not actually exist, and that he often exaggerated and misunderstood its character where it did exist, but, all the same, his faith justified him in his dread of any religious philosophy that made God the work of humanity rather than humanity the work of God. Thus he wrote, in a letter to Tyrrell of April 16th, 1908,[1] that he had been troubled by certain expressions of Loisy in his volume *Quelques Lettres*.

I don't like (he says) that sort of *anima mundi* position ... with spirit and matter at bottom the same thing, and this without any conviction as to the latter being secondary to the former. I have told him that, to me, the 'Grand Individu' idea, which is clearly his, as it is Hébert's nightmare, seems to me, compared with that, a venial error.[1]

Now for Loisy the problem was not a painful one as it was for the Baron and for many besides him, whose faith in a personal God is the one bridge that swings over an abyss reaching from a dim beginning to a hidden end. Loisy says in one place:

Neither the personality of God, nor the immortality of man, has ever been a subject of disquietude to me.... If I have sometimes speculated on the subject it has been rather for the sake of others... than for my own peace; while for von Hügel the question has never ceased to be a torturing nightmare.[2]

One cannot but note in these words the expression of a certain cold intellectuality; his feelings were not involved, as were those of his friend, and in regard, not only to the conception of God, but to the belief in a future life he professed a total detachment from all desire for personal immortality which everyone cannot share.

A little further he uncovers the root cause of his 'agnosticism, if agnosticism it be'. For

the conceptions which were compatible with the philosophy of a universe bounded in space, and historically limited in time, do not fit with what we now know or behold of an immense universe, of its freedom from historical limitation, of the past of the earth and of humanity.[3]

[1] Von Hügel, *Selected Letters*, p. 149.
[2] *Mém.* III, 23–24.   [3] *Idem*, p. 24.

And so with him, as with all of us, it is Copernicanism, with its lesson of the smallness and the apparent unimportance of the earth and the race that inhabits it, that confounds the simpler interpretation of human history.

And he wrote elsewhere:

The proofs of the existence of God, at least as regards the existence of a God eternal, unchangeable, omniscient, omnipotent, do not seem to me conclusive. Something is; therefore something has always been. But what reason cannot demonstrate, what, indeed, it can only begin to conceive with great difficulty, is the idea of a principle of evolution not immanent in the world, but transcendent to the point of possessing infinite being, independently of the universe which it created.[1]

'Something is; therefore something has always been'; in this short phrase the great problem is poignantly stated, but not necessarily better solved by the conception of a universe enfolding its own destiny than by the belief in a Power outside that universe. And, after all, man has no test of his own man-made instruments of investigation beyond that of his own mind and experience. He looks far beyond his own *habitat*, but has only his own inventions to guide him.

The Baron was right in charging Loisy with a repugnance for the 'Grand Individu' idea; but while acknowledging that he has, in fact, a difficulty in regard to that conception, he 'does not admit that God is an abstract formula, He is more real than we are'.[2]

The Baron should have been comforted by this assertion, though I fear he was not. But I cannot help asking myself whether the question between them would not have been more satisfactorily treated had they asked each other not '*what* is God?' an unanswerable question, but '*where* is God?' or, rather, *where* do we, *where* can we find Him?

I cannot help recalling a word of Paul Desjardins' on this subject; he had an intimate belief in God, but said that God was not for discussion. I remember also a remark of George Tyrrell, after a learned conference of the L.S.S.R.; he said

---

[1] *Choses Passées*, p. 313.   [2] *Mém.* III, 22.

he was seized with a sense of a certain comical element, from the point of view of the Almighty, in a small group discussion on His existence.

And I recall a word of the Baron himself, in earlier days, before his period of reaction. He had introduced me to a work of Rudolf Eucken, *Der Kampf um einen geistigen Lebensanhalt*, and when I remarked to him that there seemed to be no direct mention of God, he replied that this was because Eucken would feel that the use of the word implied certain theological conceptions which he could not accept.

Thus the refusal to define may result in the refusal to affirm, but neither refusal should be classed as denial.

Thus Loisy writes:

To his last day von H. will struggle against this phantom of absolute immanentism, and imagine that I am possessed by it....

I certainly cannot lodge his Transcendent in my mind as an indispensable guest; it is equally true that I do not imagine the human ideal to be founded on nothing. First of all, this common ideal of humanity is transcendent in relation to each separate individual; furthermore, it corresponds to the profound law or reality of the universe, which makes it transcend humanity. But is it consequently necessary to conceive this profound reality as the metaphysical object of religion, as the metaphysical custodian of morality, as a reality superior and exterior to the universe itself?...I do not know this, I do not see it, I do not understand it.[1]

On this point we can get nothing further from the subject of this study; he was convinced of a spiritual reality which transcended sense and reason, which was apprehended, but not defined, by the faith of mankind; and he asked no definition; he thought, indeed, that definitions were often destructive of spiritual faith. He asks why, if von Hügel admits that his conception of the transcendent is open to criticism and improvement, he wants to impose it on others.

'Why does he not look to see whether others may not get a glimpse of the transcendent of to-morrow?'[2]

[1] *Mém.* III, 107.   [2] *Idem*, p. 155.

And yet he persistently defended the sincerity and the faith of those for whom the old traditional doctrines remained the best and truest spiritual support and sustenance. He had no use for fancy religions, or irreligions, and, as he wrote to Paul Desjardins, on August 8th, 1909:

The religion of social duty seems to me to have at present more theologians than apostles, which is not promising for its future. . . . I am not sure that the human masses may not some day be capable of escaping from the enlightened people who want to save them by Science, and of casting themselves in desperation into superstitions very inferior to the religion they are now in the process of losing.[1]

And elsewhere:

Confounding the eternal faith of mankind with the beliefs that he had seen perish, the sceptic imagined that he had done with faith when he had 'carefully rolled her up in the purple shroud of dead gods'.[2]

All our knowledge is frail and limited, and not only religious knowledge.

If mankind seem to have advanced but by tiny steps in the general order of life and of faith, the same is true of science, and the two orders are not separate as some scientists think. Nor can it be said that science absorbs faith and will eventually suppress it; it is rather science that is enfolded by faith, outside which it could not subsist, on which it can cast light, but which it can never supplant.[3]

And in another place, again referring to von Hügel, he says:

Is it the conscience, however vague and obscure, of an absolute that gives a true and social value to the magico-religious cults of the uncivilized? Is it the clearer consciousness of this absolute which creates a human discipline in national religions? . . . Is it the transcendent that constitutes the moral value of Christianity? . . . Is not true transcendency a movement transcending its particular manifestations in immensity?

. . . . . .

Gods, whether transcendent or not. . . only become insupportable to the faithful when the mind can no longer conceive

[1] *Mém.* III, 144–145.   [2] *La Discipline Intellectuelle*, p. 139.
[3] *Idem*, p. 81.

them. Then other images, not less august, present themselves in support of human idealism, which is, in sum, the eternal religion.[1]

It was not the immanentism of conscience, nor the immanentism of the spiritual life in every human soul that was the matter of contention between von Hügel and Loisy. Whatever God was He was not for the one, any more than for the other, the creation of man or of humanity. But in the mind of von Hügel the personal conception held a prominent place; the whole attitude of his soul responded to it. For Loisy, who, we must remember, had been much more soaked in traditional theology than his friend, that personal conception was inextricably interwoven with definitions and assertions that seemed to him not the work of faith but of reason.

And this is where von Hügel totally failed to understand him, and by his misunderstanding provoked stronger negative assertions on the part of his friend.

For Loisy every religion was a recognition of reality, but it was also a scheme of spiritual knowledge, cast into the forms of doctrine and dogma. And then reason came into play, and with reason came the limitation of the human mind when it sets out to deal with ultimate reality. His quarrel with theology was that it failed in respect for the unknowable, and to fail in respect for the unknowable was to fail in respect for the unknown.

Man (he wrote elsewhere) is an animal that thinks itself intelligent. So he is, in some manner and to some degree, otherwise he could never suppose himself to be such. But he claims too much, being always ready to illude himself and exaggerate his own mental power and the extent and solidity of his knowledge.[2]

Loisy's own particular branch of knowledge was history, it was by his historical work that he had earned exclusion from the Church to which he belonged, but he does not omit history in his indictment of the exaggerated claims of the human reason. There too 'erudition may become trash if the erudite himself fails to find and show that his discoveries have a human

[1] *Mém.* III, 156–157. [2] *La Discipline Intellectuelle*, p. 5.

sense';[1] which means that the mere bare facts are not complete facts without a deeper setting.

Intelligence itself is chiefly a response, on the part of a being capable of such response, to the centre in which he finds himself. Why and how is he thus susceptible?

'To ask this is to ask the why and how of spirit in the world, to ask, in fact, for the solution of the mystery of the universe.'[2]

This is surely an expression, not of immanentism, not of pure humanism, but of a faith in the transcendent which refuses all reasoned definition. The 'mystery of the Universe' is apprehended by faith and not by reason, and it is in the apprehension of that mystery that sound scepticism and faith can meet and embrace—scepticism, which realizes the limitations of human knowledge, in dealing with unfathomed truths; and faith, which is the sense and possession of those truths, and which is more certain of them than reason is certain of its scientific conclusions.

To sum up the question as it presented itself to von Hügel on the one side, to Loisy on the other, we have, in the former, the traditional faith of Christianity resisting all efforts to dislodge it. We have the protest of a devout mind against a religious philosophy that would seem to undermine the intimate personal relations of the soul with God; a teaching so contrary, for instance, to that of Newman with his sense of the *solus cum solo* communication of himself with God. We have the dread of any substitution of man, or humanity, or the whole universe, for God.

We have, on the other side, Loisy's horror of absolutism and exclusiveness in belief, whether religious or scientific. We have his deep sense of the bewildering problem presented by the doctrine of God as Creator and external Governor of the world. We have his positivist determination that man cannot be more than human, and can only arrive at truth through human means. Any description of God seemed to him an intrusion of reason into the domain of faith. But this was not to deny divine reality, nor the mystical perception thereof.

[1] *La Discipline Intellectuelle*, p. 47.   [2] *Idem*, p. 58.

CHAPTER X

MYSTICAL HUMANITY

HUMANITY was not then for Loisy the 'Grand Être'; it was
not, in its collectivity, an object of worship; and yet it was in
and through humanity, in and through human society, that
the true object of worship was apprehended. And if he was
sparing in the use of the name of God, this was not because
he denied Him, but because he denied the adequacy of any
definition of Him. 'I do not regard God as an abstract formula.
He is more real than we are. But I think it is unwise to regard
Him too much as a *grand Individu*.'[1]

But humanity is not made, it is a thing of growth and development—and this is why no religion can be final since humanity
itself is not final. But in the process of evolution there are two
great factors—religion, of which faith is the organ; morality,
of which rightful progress is the result.

'From all that precedes', says Loisy in the fifth chapter of
La Morale Humaine, 'it is abundantly clear that the true field
of the moral life is our social existence.'[2] As he maintained,
in answer to an objection of von Hügel, he did not identify
morality and religion even though he regarded them as inseparable, holding, as he did, that man cannot see further than
human sight and human thought, and that no one can live
outside that human society into which he is inevitably born;
he also held that both religion and morality were essentially
social in character. And, indeed, I think that many are unconscious of that total dependence on society because it is,
like the air we breathe, so all embracing that we are unaware
of its continual influence on our every thought and action.
Can we conceive of any individual, in a state of complete
isolation, as self-sufficing in either religion or morality? Just
as it weakens religious faith to live amongst those who have

[1] *Mém.* III, 22.   [2] *La Morale Humaine*, p. 91.

none, and as it strengthens faith to live with those who have it, so should we none of us deny God if every human being believed in Him; and could we believe in Him if every human being denied Him?

After all, Christianity, the most dogmatic religion of all, is based on a social conception. As Loisy himself says:

> According to Christian belief Jesus, the immortal Christ, is the Saviour, the Head, the divine Soul of the Church. This Christ is not the Galilean prophet who was crucified under Pontius Pilate. He is, by rigid definition, the spirit of the universal community of believers, a type of humanity at once human and divine; a type first created by the faith of the earliest followers under the personal influence of Jesus, under the influences which had formed Jesus Himself and which reigned in certain Jewish centres of His time, and finally under the influences introduced into the new sect by recruits from paganism. . . . This type is, above all, the ideal personification of Christian society itself, which is held to subsist in Christ and to live through Him, each believer being a member of the Church, an element of the mystical body of Christ, a personal fraction of the great moral personality which is Christ in the Church and through the Church. That type is only real to faith, but it is realized in a measure through faith, and becomes living and active in the society of believers. And this society is the more intimate and consistent and durable, the more perfectly human, in so far as its type, its ideal and its spirit are the more profoundly moral. Christ is the Christian ideal, the moral and social centre of the faithful.[1]

And yet, he says, in the same book, that Christianity 'is not yet, and may never become, the religion of humanity, because the human mentality is not yet formed'; and it could only realize that end by 'radical transformation',[2] of which transformation he neither predicts nor denies the possibility, but of which the character must be human in the most universal sense.

Christianity has not become the moral system nor the religion of humanity, it can only become such by radically transforming itself and abandoning its claim to be a special and absolute

---

[1] *La Morale Humaine*, pp. 109–111.
[2] *Idem*, p. 39.

revelation. Yet it represents undeniably the greatest and most successful effort that has yet been made for the moral elevation of humanity.[1]

And he points out that this effort has been made, not in accordance with the existing economy of society, but in opposition to it. Like Buddhism, it was an effort to achieve the impossible, but an effort which succeeded, nevertheless, in proclaiming a new human discipline, whose effects were salutary. It achieved this result by its promise of eternal life, a promise which Loisy terms a myth, but a myth containing more truth than the Buddhist message of annihilation or rest. But its moral progress has been halted by its immobility and absolutism, by its tenacity of the past and refusal to recognize the present, with its needs and fresh ideals. For:

Humanity bursts through the frames of Christian evangelization and Christian belief.... But Christianity has prepared more efficaciously than any other religion the advent of human religion, the reign of humanity.[2]

Another point, on which he expresses what he considers to be a weakness of the Christian message, is its promise of future happiness as the reward of present goodness. He says:

To make happiness dependent on an unverifiable hope, as does Christianity . . . is to deny, in fact, the reality of happiness for man, and to mistake the true character of human morality.[3]

And yet, further on, he says:

There is a kind of Messianism in the normal conditions of life. Although we have brought our hopes closer, and although the object of our endeavour is conceived in terms of possibility and not of fantasy, we still live to a great extent in the future, even if we no longer take the risk of eternity.[4]

Loisy is resolute in his exclusion of all that cannot be based on any form of human experience; that experience includes, certainly, the experience of faith as well as reason, but it does not include any unproved message from beyond, nor any

[1] *La Morale Humaine*, p. 124.
[2] *Idem*, p. 219.
[3] *Idem*, p. 277.
[4] *Idem*, p. 285.

unproved hope for the future. Yet he lands us on the threshold of mystery; as for religious faith so for morality.

True practical morality is founded on a mystical conception of the universe, and still more of humanity, whether human society or individual man.[1]

And so we come to the dividing point between his spiritual philosophy and the traditional faith of Christianity, as also of Judaism. He will not seek outside humanity for the source of the spiritual faith of humanity; he will not look outside the past history of the human race nor outside its future possibilities for the meaning and explanation of its spiritual destiny, while Christianity boldly declares that the message comes from beyond, and that there is a continued action on man from beyond.

But if he will not look beyond humanity, and its past and present testimony, for the proof of something greater than humanity, he persistently recognizes the impact on mankind of something greater than man can comprehend. Every religion is, for him, the expression of faith in this unseen, undefinable mystery. Faith was no mere accident of human life, and it could not have persisted throughout the long history of mankind without a cause which was inherent to human life. Religions have been coarse and brutal, and yet they have something in common with the most spiritual types. They have been racial and national, and yet there has been in them something that could not be confined to the barriers of race and nation. They have fluctuated and varied, and this for the reason that they are always, in a measure, experimental, 'an experimental order of existence'. The apostles of reason have failed to see that 'humanity is in the process of becoming, she has begun and she will continue indefinitely'; the learned themselves only achieve 'a slight effort in the pursuit of that truth which they flatter themselves to possess in its entirety'.[2]

The true exponents of religion are the religious; political considerations are a falsification of its ends.[3] And, in the same

---

[1] *La Morale Humaine*, p. 33.   [2] *La Religion*, p. 79.
[3] *Idem*, p. 25.

way, it is the saints and the heroes who could explain religion and morality if only they had been moved to describe the secret of their sanctity.[1]

'Faith is essentially an indestructible sense of confidence in life and in its moral value',[2] and nothing great can be done in the world without faith in humanity.

All men are called to the service of that living and growing human ideal, and the most criminal and unpardonable heresy is to disbelieve in it.[3]

And as faith is the response to the mysterious truth of the universe, so morality is, in its deepest sense, the direction of human conduct to the fulfilment of the human ideal.

Human morality

does not spring from personal speculations, nor from rational or scientific experience, but from a more profound sentiment . . . that of solidarity, of the bond which binds the individual to family and society making him member of a body on which the whole of his life . . . is dependent. This sentiment may well be that of the essential relation which exists between the law of humanity and the law of the universe. Whencesoever this sentiment may arise, and whithersoever it may tend, whatsoever may be its primary root and its completion in the infinite, it does not owe its origin to humanity.[4]

But if man is essentially social, if a separated individual would be spiritually lifeless and impotent, that same individual has his part, in society, for society.

Human truth is neither purely individual nor purely social, it is both. . . . Individuals are the organs as well as the channels of truth . . . the social character stands for religion and truth, the individual note is that of liberty.

Society must not be conceived as a collection of numbers, but as a living whole, and thus through the cult of humanity the soul of each one penetrates to the cult of what is greater than humanity, to the cult of universal and supreme being—

[1] *La Religion*, p. 47.
[2] *Idem*, p. 181.
[3] *La Discipline Intellectuelle*, p. 179.
[4] *Idem*, p. 10.

'to that domain of the unknown, which is the profound sense of universal being'.[1]

This is the mystery of eternal life, the mystery of God, if we keep this word. This is the mystery which conditions our nature, and, as we may say along with old theologians, which gives merit to our faith.[2]

It is only too clear that natural science is quite insufficient for the direction of human progress. . . . human progress needs a light to be thrown upon its path and this can come only from those branches of science which deal with humanity,

and

Religion is an element or an aspect of human life, it is the aspect or mystical form of life in the individual and in society; it is the great human fact of the past as of the present.[3]

In every form of belief, whether religious or scientific, there is indeed an element of illusion; more patent in religion, but present also in science. But such illusion is as inevitable as it is significant.

Mystical illusion results apparently from the impression produced on man by the universe which surrounds and seems to dominate him; and this impression is the deeper and more poignant because of his sense of utter powerlessness. *But this illusion is only such by reason of the infirmity of our nature*; for it is actually an *experience*, and it is through the weakness of our reason that the intellectual definition of this experience proves incorrect. But man is quick to define because he wants to act; and because his definitions up to a point control his actions.[4]

And to conclude with words from the *Essais* quoted in the *Mémoires*:

Perhaps the theology of the coming centuries will be more cautious than that of the past; will be less confident in the permanent value of formulas and will seek light in the very obscurity of faith rather than in the fragile constructions of reason. Such wisdom will in itself mark a progress, and under its influence divine revelation, human redemption and the

[1] *La Discipline Intellectuelle*, p. 42.
[2] *Idem*, p. 119.
[3] *Religion et Humanité*, pp. 72–76.
[4] *Idem*, p. 136. (My own italics—M.D.P.)

socialization of men in the religion of Christ will be perfected and perpetuated, finding perhaps wider and more spiritual expressions through a more direct consciousness of the law that governs their evolution.[1]

And he wrote to the Baron himself:

The religious evolution of humanity is an absolutely strange phenomenon. To see in it just the history of human folly is the height of unintelligence. For the history of religion is the history of what is most vital and essentially human, the development of moral life. The force underlying this development may be mysterious, but it is something other than an inexhaustible source of contradictions. Religion and human sociability have a solidarity of interest, and human progress is just the religious sense of humanity, a sense that is ever growing but that destroys itself as soon as it denies its mystical character.[2]

In this he was akin to a Christian apologist, of his own country, whom he never met, but whom he greatly desired to meet.[3] Both of them sought in the history of the earth and of humanity the message of hope and spiritual progress. For this other there is a Spirit of Humanity as there is a spirit in every man; and his 'Human Front' has, for its task, the development of that common spirit, as a Popular Front seeks the good of a particular people.

He is no mere theorist, no idealist, but a man of science, who has explored the dark regions of pre-history and the origin of life; and it is from the deep beginnings of life and conscience that he draws the proof of man's spiritual destiny. But it is a common destiny; not merely the salvation of each one's soul; and it is a destiny which must be recognized in order to be fulfilled. Even now it is pursued by mankind at large, but blindly, gropingly; so blindly and gropingly that men bite and scratch each other in the dark—unable to distinguish friend from foe; still more unable to see that all, at bottom, need the same thing.

---

[1] *Mém.* I, 463.   [2] *Idem*, III, 332.
[3] Teilhard de Chardin—a priest and a palaeontologist.

And so the task before us is one of search, search for the discovery of a New World, but whose newness will not consist in an addition of territory, but in a transformation of shape. For the shape of a thing alters as we look at it from one point or another, as we consider it in relation to one environment or another. We have been gazing on our world of humanity piecemeal; we have to regard it as a whole.

Perhaps (Teilhard says), urged by the need to construct the unity of the world, we shall come to perceive that the great work, which science has pursued and obscurely foreseen, is nothing else than the discovery of God.

There is so much kinship between these thoughts and those of Loisy that one wishes the two men could have met and exchanged ideas. The writer quoted above lays more stress on the message of natural science, and Loisy more on the study of humanity itself, but for both there is the same question 'Where is God?' and for both He transcends the place in which He is found.

Our faith (writes Loisy) is not in the human race as such, nor in our frail individualities, it is in the spirit which leads and the ideal which raises humanity. 'Faith', says the author of the Epistle to the Hebrews, 'is the substance of things hoped for, the evidence of things not seen.' It is the pressure of the spirit on humanity. It is the intimate force which draws humanity to what is better, not only in the realm of knowledge, but in the whole order of spiritual life. Reason explains and orders—sometimes narrows and stifles—these living intuitions of the soul. We cannot do without it, for its function is to regulate our external life and the current of our experience. Humanity is not so fashioned as to plunge into the ideal and to live wholly in the spirit; it is reason that gives them practical usage. She gives them their form in religious beliefs, moral laws, legislations, art and industry. But it is not reason that sustains and animates all these things. The profoundly mystical, living and spiritual sense which carries men forward, as it were against themselves, that sense so often failing, but never conquered, is the eternal faith, the intuition of infinite life which we behold as it were in a vision and seek to realize.

.   .   .   .   .   .

If the peoples of the earth ever come to form one family it will not be through reason alone . . . it will be when they conceive and experience the same mystic ideal of universal solidarity, when they embrace, all together, the religion of humanity.[1]

One of the greatest Christian teachers had foretold that tongues should cease, and doctrine should fade away, when faith finds its culmination in charity. But this cannot be as yet. And for Loisy, in spite of all that was negative in his assertions, faith did hold its office of spiritual antennae, responding to unseen and undefined reality.

Has religious faith ever been anything else than a trusting adherence to a human ideal, small or great, to the realization of which faith contributes in an appreciable measure? Is not faith one of the most powerful and necessary factors of human progress? . . .

It is not faith that has invented superstitions, theological systems, orthodoxies and the suppression of thought by the Inquisition; it is reason, a reason . . . too sure of itself. . . . Scholastic theologians have been, and many still are, fierce rationalists, like their counterparts, the absolute theorists of science and reason.[2]

This same anti-rationalism, if we may thus describe it, explains how Loisy could respect the simple faith of the Catholic peasant; the ardent but unquestioning devotion of religious and nuns, as presented in his friend Henri Brémond's work; and also the dim gropings of the savage mind in early religions, with their blend of magic.

For, reading back into human origins he found, under all myths and figments, under all the aberrations of magic and superstition, a universal sense of a spiritual force, the response of the human soul to the mystery of the universe.

He protests against science as he had protested against theology, for the needs of the many. 'For my meat shall the weak brother perish for whom Christ died.' There are illusions that are a mere perversion of truth, but there are also illusions that are dim guesses at a truth too great for our comprehension.

[1] *Religion et Humanité*, pp. 111, 112, 113, 114.
[2] *Idem*, pp. 218–219.

I append the following letter to myself, which bears on the same subject:

Paris, December 1st, 1918.

This time your precious gift arrived safely. Many thanks for all. The volume on Modernism is,[1] to my mind, historically irreproachable. I say no more, because all books on Modernism, even good ones, affect me like a funeral oration, and it is as though my ashes were being raked. I think that the Modernist movement has borne its fruits and if it is renewed, and it certainly will be, it will be from another point of departure, it will not be our modernism.[2]

Your little book on Democracy pleased me greatly.[3]

It corresponds to the present situation of my country, but I should like to see it translated into the tongues of all civilized nations, and first of all into French. It contains a summary of just and clear ideas, well presented. They should be displayed in large letters in every Parliament, in every electoral assembly. . . .

I have been struck by the exactitude with which you have understood and summarized my book *La Religion.* But allow me certain reservations on the final reflections. I remain sceptical in regard to the necessary consideration of a metaphysical beyond in the institution of religion. The cult of this impenetrable beyond becomes impossible when one perceives the universal inadequacy—I was going to say the *incompetence*—of every idea or definition in its regard. The mystico-moral consideration of humanity does not explain the universe, but it suffices for the foundation of duty. It cannot be denied that we owe humanity as much evil as good; but this objection is rather valid *contra Deum.* Humanity did not make itself; it struggles with a native infirmity for which it is not really responsible. Besides, the faith one has in it implies faith in the undefinable and incomprehensible in the progress of life, of conscience and of morality. I do not deny this principle, but I should feel that I was insulting it by imagining that I could express it in a formula or treat with it as an equal. . . . Revelation, as you understand it, is not what the Catholic Church teaches. I have never denied that revelation, which is the reflex of a

---

[1] *Modernism, its failure and its fruits.*
[2] The sentence that follows seems unfinished.
[3] *Democracy at the cross roads.*

profound and unfathomable reality in the struggle of humanity towards goodness; but it is equivocal to present this conception as that of the Scriptures and of Catholic tradition. I employ the term *religion* without scruple, because it has a wide sense and covers the mystico-moral evolution of humanity. But the word revelation has a much narrower sense as the revelation of dogma, Jewish or Christian, which has not been revealed in the proper sense of the word—*intuition* would be a more correct term provided you added as many adjectives as were necessary to limit its sense. You suppose, very gratuitously, that the religion of humanity can only be commemorative. It would be so in the measure of every religion, but not more so. Faith in humanity assumes its present and future as much as its past; its symbols and rites would have an object as wide as its faith, and they would act in the same way as ancient religious symbols. I do not deny mystical experience, but I behold it so varied and confused that it seems to me to confirm the incomprehensible and undefinable character of its object. The renewal of the consciousness of our relation to humanity would be as uplifting[1] as the claim to find in ourselves the moral force which we need; it would be an effort to attain and realize the permanent truth and devotion that move and grow in humanity. It is another question whether it be better to remain united to the Catholic Communion or to separate from it in order to realize human progress. There are arguments for and against both hypotheses; in some cases the separation is unavoidable. Without drawing therefrom an argument against yourself I note the fact that the Church does not hesitate to regard as strangers those who do not admit the absolute value of the symbols and the imperialism of her doctrine and authority. The religion that you defend is more like the religion of humanity than real authentic Catholicism.

.   .   .   .

[1] Here I hope to have found the correct word as two of those in the letter are hard to decipher.

CHAPTER XI

THE FUTURE OF HUMANITY

I HOPE that what has gone before, and the testimony of Loisy's own words, will have shown that, for him, the moral and spiritual future of men depended on religion. Without religion humanity would tend downwards rather than upwards, because without religion men would lose faith, and it was through faith that they apprehended the secret and the meaning of the universe.

Could men utterly renounce religion and close their ears to the message of faith? I think he would have replied that the whole history of the human race proved that such a total denial was, collectively, impossible, although phases of spiritual dullness and deafness might intervene, when men would either be forgetful of their own high destiny, or would sink back into gross forms of superstitious belief.

There was something ineradicably apostolic in his mind and soul, and the state of human society after the war filled him alternately with hope and misgiving. He carried on his exegetical labours to the end of his life, and, as I have said throughout, it is not with those works that I deal. But his mind was always working beyond this professional occupation, and his spiritual searchings and anxieties inspired those shorter works from which I have so largely quoted.

These were not books of prayer or devotion; they were not treatises of doctrine; they contained arguments neither for nor against the Christian faith in its essence. They were the work of one who believed that the essence of every spiritual faith was as imperishable as it was, from the human point of view, vitally necessary, and that it would and must survive all the vicissitudes of human knowledge and belief. Every form of belief must adjust itself to the movement of human life, and, if it survived, it was because it was truly alive. Hence his impatience with rationalistic dogmatism, whether theological or scientific. Hence also, in spite of many crudely sceptical criticisms, his recurring tributes to the force of the Christian faith. It was not its essential message that had failed; it was the apparent immobility of the Christian Church that made him despair of its future.

But in regard to humanity itself, and its true ideals, there must be no 'defeatism', no despair of its future.

'No great work can be accomplished in this world save by those with faith in mankind.'[1]

And religion is nothing else than faith in mankind, which implies faith in something higher and greater than mankind, but present to mankind; while morality, the inseparable co-worker with religion, is, in its essence, the effort of man to pursue, though never to fulfil, the spiritual ideal of faith.

And so it is false and injurious to human hopes to maintain that we have gone as far as we can go; humanity is not made, but is ever in the making. We have not reached the end, and 'The cry of the disillusioned sceptic: "O abyss, thou art the only god" is a lie in the face of humanity.'[2]

But, for the same reason, the immobility of religious doctrine and belief is a denial of the human process.

He was very conscious that a merely philosophical spirituality was not adequate or efficient; that faith must find some organ of sanction. This was why he upheld the need of existing religions and almost angrily repudiated purely destructive efforts in their regard. We may recall his warning me against accepting an invitation to the celebration of his own Jubilee until he had assured himself that it would not have an anti-clerical, sectarian character.

But every religion perverted its true end by imposing a *ne plus ultra* of spiritual effort; however high and holy, it should ever be preparatory of something higher and holier, and this it could not be if it suppressed or excluded the rightful movements of human life. He believed that Christianity was hitherto the highest religious effort, but any claim to finality was a

[1] *La Religion*, p. 187.   [2] *Idem*, p. 315.

non-human claim. He was no religion maker, but his faith in religion, as the true embodiment of human life and hope, was grounded on the fact that it survived every passing form of belief.

The evil of dogmatic unbelief is that it weakens the spring of moral force; . . . whatever may be said to the contrary men are not happy as sheep without shepherds, and the shepherds they have always followed most readily are not those who have talked of science, or even of liberty, but those who have preached duty and sacrifice.[1]

And in another passage from the same work he says:

The trust of long ages in that eternal life, whose source is in the heart of humanity, is not like a long chain that can be broken at will and its fragments cast into a pit; that same trust constitutes the inexhaustible force that sustains the human race on its sad pilgrimage. How short-sighted are the learned who think they have found out that this sentiment of confidence in life, a sentiment which is essentially religious, has no other object than that physical life whose preservation they endeavour to facilitate. Trust in life is trust in social life, in spiritual life, in moral life, in the ascent of humanity towards an ever greater ideal of truth and goodness.[2]

And again:

Without gods, without prayer, mankind are lost; and does not this very need, does not this failure prove the necessity of prayer and the reality of divine help, at least in the order of interior life, of conscience, of morality? Prayer has helped man, and prayer is necessary to him. It is equally evident that man has not drawn this help from himself; it is not from some secret individual resource that he has drawn this force, but from the treasure of religious tradition, from the ideal of divine humanity. . . . It is in this living ideal that is the force that has come to those who have invoked it, and in whom it has become incarnate by prayer.[3]

Can man do without this ideal? he asks in another place. Is religion doomed to disappear?

[1] *La Discipline Intellectuelle*, p. 143.   [2] *Idem*, p. 140.
[3] *Idem*, p. 276.

No, he would answer—not if humanity be as great as we believe it to be.

Religions have never been simply systems of arbitrary be-lief. . . they have been, above all, the mystical and transcendent form of social life; the ideal that consecrated that life, and sought realization in it. . . .

In the anguish and disturbance of the present time this ideal seems to be largely forgotten; one might say that economic interests predominate. . . .

But man does not live on bread alone, though he cannot do without it. He aspires to more than material advantages though he lets himself be absorbed in them. He must nourish his soul also, and how is he to do it?[1]

And here we have the expression of that persistent post-war preoccupation of his mind with the spiritual needs of mankind. One may suffer, and suffer acutely, and, please God, no one is incapable of such suffering, at the sight or thought of physical pain; of starvation and torture. And when such pain is wide-spread, intense and insistent it is difficult to think of anything else. But although such suffering be more immediate; although we cannot rest in our own lives when other lives are being wrung out and destroyed; there may be as great, and an even more enduring cause for sorrow in the thought of the spiritual starvation of the multitude; in the vision of a world deprived of its hopes and ideals—'they have taken away my Lord and I know not where they have laid him'.

But it is in the darkest hours that the brave will reject all counsels of defeatism and despair; and spiritual defeatism is surely more finally disastrous and deadly than its physical or national counterpart.

But the spiritual faith of mankind can never take a holiday, can never settle itself in a final resting place. Movement is our destiny, as of the individual soul so of all human society.

If the moral effort of every religion has proved inadequate, if every religion has had its decline, it is because ever new efforts are needed to create or renew religion for the incorpora-tion of that faith that never dies.

[1] *Religion et Humanité*, pp. 8, 9.

But such effort will never be made save through mystical faith in the future of humanity.[1]

A deeper knowledge of living reality does not wipe out its mystery...rational illusion is not less dangerous than mystical illusion.

We are no enemies of reason, we are no enemies of religion: 'we seek our way in the night', trusting that the humblest effort will not be wholly vain.[2]

But that faith in humanity, without which nothing can be achieved, is not

faith in the human race as such, in our feeble personalities, but in the spirit which informs and uplifts humanity. 'Faith is the substance of things hoped for, the evidence of things not seen.' Faith is the pressure of the spirit on humanity; it is the intimate force that impels humanity towards what is better, not only in the order of knowledge but in the whole order of the spiritual life.[3]

From another standpoint like thoughts were being uttered by Teilhard, of whom I have already spoken. He is dealing with those pessimistic prophets for whom the world is moving, not forwards but backwards, and is rather sinking back to chaos than advancing to a fuller and higher life.

They recall past catastrophes; they enumerate the physical and moral proofs of decadence. Mere short-sightedness! we may reply. Replace these startling facts in the universal phenomenon. Their irregularity becomes insignificant in relation to the majestic, steady and unfailing movement of the whole. Life has conquered or reversed all the obstacles that she has hitherto encountered....In spite of all contrary evidence we may and should believe that we are advancing.

It is, in fact, through his study of the Past that this thinker is a believer in the Future. Seeing the steady emergence of light from darkness, of order from confusion, of mind from matter; seeing that the process has been continuous through all interruptions, he does not believe in its coming to an end

---

[1] *Religion et Humanité*, pp. 167–168.
[2] *Idem*, pp. 169–170.   [3] *Idem*, pp. 111–112.

just because we, of the year 1936 (date of the essay from which I quote), are confounded with one of the evil turns in the process of life.

Teilhard believes, then, in the Future, and he asks what is the kind of Future to which man, as a conscious being, must ever tend.

The first of those conditions is that the Future should offer us an open and *unlimited* horizon.... No progress can truly interest us unless we go forward without fear of being arrested in our march. The Reality towards which Man tends must be incorruptible and inexhaustible.

Too vast to allow of any barrier to possible development, the Future must also be so comprehensive as to exclude no positive element of the Universe. Totality, after Limitlessness, this is the second character, without which the Future could not content human hope. I appeal to the evidence of each one's kind.... This demand for universality is stamped on every soul....

Far back as we may go in the history of philosophy and religion, the idea of a Whole in process of formation has always been the magnetic Pole of the highest intelligences and the noblest souls.

No abstract formula could suffice—The magnet that should draw us out of the present welter of wasted energies and useless shocks is only to be found in the disclosure of some essential object, whose splendour, outshining gold and all other beauty, would be for man, now risen to his full stature, the Grail or Eldorado of which ancient conquerors dreamed; a concrete object, for the possession of which life could well be sacrificed.

It is the fact that they were contemporaries, that they knew of each other, and that Loisy himself, as he told me, deeply regretted the fact that they had never met, which justifies me, I hope, in adding these quotations to this last study of Loisy's religious works.

For both of them it was the infinite that counted, for both of them man was, as Loisy wrote, caught between two infinities, the infinite of being and of truth, the infinite of nothingness. For both the possibilities of human progress were not to be gauged by anything yet achieved. For both the true destiny of man was spiritual and not material. For both true religion implied faith in humanity as well as faith in the end to which humanity should ever tend. The message of Teilhard is more joyful, but both messages are hopeful, and Loisy concluded his *Mémoires* with a word of confidence in human co-operation and world peace.

If he seemed indifferent to his own personal future, this was because he had no care for his own personality as separate from humanity as a whole. And it is surely that sense of separatism which is conquered by a deeper sense of universal one-ness. The Christian faith in many does not seem, at least consciously, to attain that sense of unity, and yet it is the very essence of the Christian message. It is the separatist view of individual and social life that is at the root of spiritual unbelief and despair. Regarded separately men seem often to be going backward rather than forward; regarded as living elements of the whole they can bear present suffering for they see and know, as Teilhard says, that the march of human life has been, when counted by centuries, from lower to higher. And it would not be of much moment if this were true only in the material order, but through all setbacks, even violent ones, the spiritual striving of mankind ever continues, and the ideal is never entirely lost to view.

Loisy thought he could do but little in the great cause, but he knew that no efforts are unavailing, and he worked to the end at the task of spiritual regeneration.

The human race has existed for a long time, but humanity has yet to be created. . . . The ideal is plain even in the midst of the greatest peril, it inspires the vision and hopes of a race that seeks to live.[1]

[1] *La Morale Humaine*, p. 216.

CHAPTER XII

THE SIGNIFICANCE OF LOISY

HAVING come to the end of this study I shall endeavour to
summarize, if only for my own mind, but hoping it may be to
some extent for other minds also, the significance of his life
and thought in the religious order.

We know that he has been one of the authorities on Scriptural
exegesis, and, for some, it is his work in that field, and that
work alone, which is of interest. And for some it is even the
negative and destructive elements of that work that are of
the most importance.

Now I have said that I do not enter on any technical discussion of those works, because it is beyond my competence.
But I will venture to say as much as this, viz. that even in those
critical works there is a religious spirit at work, and that his
abiding study of Christian documents was motived by his
belief in their paramount importance for the history of mankind. And I venture to think that, except amongst those who
actually desire to destroy Christian evidence, as mischievous
to the thought of mankind, there must be some sense of their
value in the spiritual order. Otherwise those few documents
would not have occupied the minds and time of so many first-
rank historians.

Then, of course, his first interest in exegesis was definitely
religious; and his first critical work was intended for the use
and enlightenment of Catholic students.

I do not think this earlier phase of life and thought can be
properly understood without a study of the first volume of his
Mémoires, in which he gives a synopsis of his *Livre Inédit*: a very
genuine Christian apology.

Of course he repudiated this work later, and was quite
determined against its publication; and yet he preserved much
of it in his *Mémoires*, which is significant. I have witnessed

in others than Loisy an almost mischievous pleasure in condemning past work which no longer represented their mental attitude; but sometimes that past work is not without its meaning even when it has been cast aside.

But that the religious interest survived the shock of his rupture with the Church is plain. He had no longer any ambition to be a 'Father of the Church', as he jokingly said in regard to his *Livre Inédit*, but he did endeavour to be, in humble measure, an apostle of human religion.

I remember a discussion that took place between myself and friends of mine at the Hôtel Lutetia in Paris. The two Baruzi brothers were present and Comte de Ponge. All three maintained, against my opinion, that Loisy could never pray. On my return home I submitted the dispute to Louis Canet, the most intimate of Loisy's followers. He replied that he certainly prayed, and devoted a space of time every morning to meditation.

Morally it was a life of utter purity and integrity; unworldly, unambitious; direct and truthful.

His chief fault, of which his intimate friends were very fully conscious, was his impatience of contradiction and resentfulness of criticism. A very intimate friend of his told me that he was always at pains not to show where he differed from him, and though this need not have implied deceit or subservience it did eliminate argument and opposition.

This recalls to my mind something I once read about Victor Hugo who displayed, far more arrogantly, the same characteristic. It was said, by one of his disciples, that he would not dare to whisper, even into a hole in the earth, any criticism of 'the master'.

But, on the other hand, he had the utmost respect for our convictions, and would never have said a word to weaken religious devotion of any kind.

He was a good friend, but I do not think that friendly love was as strong in him as family love. I suppose men whose chief activity is in the intellectual order are more confined in their friendships than others. We have seen how, in spite of any professions to the contrary, his differences with von Hügel weakened the bond of affection. And I, who was one of the small number that escaped the lash, cannot but regret the severity of his treatment of many friends in the *Mémoires*. He was a solitary man, living with his own thoughts, and I doubt if he ever realized the general effect of his personal criticisms. He was not proud, but he was self-centred, and inclined, in his loneliness, to brood over opposition and offence.

For the rest, it was a life of unceasing labour, without recreation or distraction, its only lighter amusement being his garden and his chickens, so long as he was physically able to work at either. He had the true Frenchman's love of the soil, and the true Frenchman's love of France. In a letter he wrote to me on February 9th, 1917, referring to some article of mine, he said:

Without insisting I will draw your attention to one point. I do not maintain that patriotism, simply as such, is an adequate and complete religion. In *Guerre et Religion* I have explained— too briefly, but still I have explained—that every country is a humanity in itself, with an ideal that tends to universality, but is sometimes very poor and narrow. The essence of my thought is that we serve mankind in the service that we render directly to those around us and to our country. . . . I have a special reason for insisting on the religion of patriotism, because it is the one ground on which the men of good will in France can meet.[1]

I never cease to be thankful that he did not live to see the France of Vichy and of Nazism, and I even wish he had left his much loved country a little sooner.

To return then to the early phase, and to that *Livre Inédit*. In spite of misgivings, which made themselves felt very early, he had high hopes for a future of work in and for the Church; he had even a definite programme, which might have filled the whole of his life. But the trouble was that he not only saw the Church, but that he also saw beyond the Church; he saw her not only in herself, but in her relation to the vast mystery of the universe.

This need not have forced a breach, for there are other big

[1] The whole of this letter is in the Appendix.

minds who, like Chesterton, if he has been rightly described to me by one who greatly believed in him, have felt that they could swing outwards into the vast field of truth without losing their anchorage in the Church. And Loisy might have done this, and instead of being a *vitandus* he might have been a great light in the Church itself. He would not have been the only one of her doctors whose thoughts, even whose words, outstripped conventional orthodoxy. He would have had his own interior sufferings, as those must have whose consciousness of mystery is keener than their consciousness of the defined truths of faith; whose faith, in fact, is wider than their belief. But such suffering need not have alienated him from the communion of the faithful, nor driven him out from his religious home.

But circumstances were unfavourable; the temper of the Church was against him, and he was not made of the stuff to temporize.

We must remember, in fairness to those who were not always fair, that the impact of historical criticism on the traditional teaching of the Church was terrifying; that it seemed a case of saving the very essence of the Christian faith from destruction. Not perhaps, since the startling revelation of Copernicanism, had the shock been greater. Loisy was prepared to help the Church to face the crisis, but he could not do it by shutting his eyes to what he regarded as facts; he could not help to suppress knowledge, but only to absorb it. Anyhow, the result of the whole sad history, which cannot be repeated here, was that he found that his work in the Church was ended.

We have seen that his work for religion was not ended, and we have seen the direction which it afterwards took. But, as a Catholic, I am furthermore interested in the question as to what elements of his teaching may be deemed to have a true and permanent value, not only for religion in general, but even for the Christian and the Catholic religion.

First of all I would place what he himself hinted at, as a solution that he could have proffered had it had a chance of acceptance. This was his conception of the New Testament literature as catechetical and not historical in character. This, of course, did not eliminate an historical background, but it did eliminate the danger to faith of total dependence on detailed historical accuracy. As someone[1] put it to me very tersely and profoundly: 'he saw that Christianity had created its literature and not been created by it'.

If those who read these lines would reflect on this suggestion they will see, I think, what a penetrating influence it might have on Christian apologetic. The other day I was idly watching the action of an aeroplane. It was flying, at first, just beneath a heavy bank of clouds; then, all at once, it plunged into a deep black one and I thought to see it disappear. But it did not. Instead it seemed to open an archway of light through the darkness, and I saw it making its way through the clarified tunnel until it passed out of sight.

It seems to me that Loisy's suggestion was like an opening pierced through the clouds of darkness that ever surround the Church, as they surround every religion on its earthly passage; and that, if the Church would accept her human destiny, she would, in virtue of her divine mission, pass unscathed through the dark tunnels to the light on the other side.

This conception of the character of the Scriptures is an intensely human conception, because it supposes the Church, like mankind, to be ever working from facts it has not created to the creation of life and truth that are based on those facts. Not a whit need it lessen the divine origin of the message, nor divine aid in the interpretation of it. On this point, as Loisy always argued, criticism is silent for the simple reason that criticism has nothing to say. And if criticism did raise its voice on such matters, then the Church had every right to beat it down by her own weapons.

Meanwhile the recognition by the Church of her own limitations in the field of human knowledge would imply the recognition that she lived on earth, and not in heaven; and that her task was with and for living men, with their living thoughts and needs; with and for humanity with its deeply buried past and its unpredictable future.

[1] Dr L. P. Jacks.

Next I would place, as a contribution to religious faith, his repudiation of all artificial myth making; that is to say, of the myth that is not an effort at the comprehension of truth, but a substitute for truth; whether the myth be the work of pious makers of fiction or of critical students of history. But, of the two types, he disliked the second the most.

And then, even on the point where many Christian believers would shrink from his views, his treatment of the person of Christ. When I listen at times to the sentimental, or hearty and jovial, presentations of the speaker's conception of Christ on the wireless I say to myself that Loisy's ruthless criticism was more reverent, and far more consonant with belief in the divinity of Christ, than those popular essays at Christian theology. And, as we have seen, he made short work of those who denied the historicity of Christ and the reality of early Christian belief.

And then, above all, his resolute effort to urge on men the spiritual character of the universe, and their own spiritual needs. He exalted men only to make them realize their own lowliness in face of the ideal towards which they should ever tend. They were not perfect, but they could do much in the order of perfectibility. And throughout all, the keynote was charity. I think he very truly, like St Thomas Aquinas, esteemed all his work as straw in comparison with the eternal interests of life.

And so I conclude my humble effort to interpret a great Frenchman to my compatriots. It is surely fitting to try to do for him what no one in his country can at present do.

I remember my last walk in his garden with him in 1938. We must both have felt that it might well be the last time, for his bodily strength was failing fast, though his mind was keen as ever. We both hoped the great tragedy might be averted— and for him, I thank God, it has been averted in its worst form. He has not seen the downfall of the country he loved, for him, as for all Frenchmen, the incarnation of humanity.

APPENDIX

PASSAGES FROM LOISY'S LETTERS

On a suggestion that I should write about a book of his.

Ceffonds, April 17th, 1914.

I have no anxiety in regard to what you may say about me. You have a perfect right to judge my opinions and my public acts, and I know that, for the rest, you will be indulgent. You do not forget that we have all suffered!

THE PRIEST AS SOLDIER

Paris, February 2nd, 1915.

Clericalism and anti-clericalism are, for the moment, arrested (*mortifiés*). May they remain so. The fraternity of military service will have a good moral effect on the clergy that are under arms, by giving them a better understanding of contemporary humanity; on the other hand, the priest himself recovers esteem and popularity. I hope that it will no longer be possible for men, that have faced such dangers in common, to be fundamentally divided; it will not be possible to imbue the clergy with fanaticism against the nation, nor to rouse the nation against the clergy. Peace with the Pope will follow as a modest consequence.

Referring to my little book *Reflections of a non-Combatant.*

October 13th, 1915.

Believe me, I had no intention of entering on a dispute—an exercise for which I have no use, and in which I should quickly lose my patience. Your book, being original in character, supplied me with matter for the discussion of certain points and the clearing of some of my own ideas. My criticism is of the form and statement of your thoughts, and not of their substance. But I did not dare to say clearly how the rigor of your logic alarms me. Between ourselves, I have always thought that a want of logic is often our best means of attaining truth . . . .

In the face of the complications inherent in the terrible events now in prospect any words we may write are quite futile—they are but as grains of sand cast into the whirlwind, making little impression on the cyclone. Of course, there is to-morrow, that famous to-morrow that is so slow in coming. But to-morrow! Material anxieties will occupy the first place, for we shall be exhausted. To-morrow will be in some ways more difficult than the present, because we shall be conscious of the gaps and ruins, while the plans for reparation will be less clear in our minds than at present, when we are faced with the need of national defence.

Paris, February 9th, 1917.

I thank you sincerely for having sent me your article.[1] All that you say is quite true, and I could sign your programme with both hands.

Without insisting, I should like to call your attention to one point. I do not hold that the cult of the Fatherland, taken simply as such, is an adequate and complete religion. In *Guerre et Religion* I have explained, briefly indeed, but still I have explained, that every country is a humanity, with its own ideal, which tends to universality, but is sometimes very low and very narrow. The substance of my thought is therefore as follows: actually, we can only serve humanity through the service that we render directly to those around us and to our country—this, so far as ordinary mortals are concerned. But there are individuals who do, in fact, directly serve civilized humanity, and whose action extends itself even to posterity; but it is always to their own country that their activities are principally directed during their lives. In principle, we pursue and serve an ideal of humanity on a line of light that broadens continually in its three elements of duty, sacrifice and love. These elements seem to me to be the foundation of every religion: in the lower forms it may be barely discernible, being as much confused as reason itself and as rudimentary as the feeble civilization of the uncivilized; in the religions of the civilized it is, in one sense or another, more clearly marked and is definitely orientated in this sense by Christianity, with its mystical synthesis of the religions of the Mediterranean world. The symbols of all the ancient theologies seem to me accessory

[1] I can only suppose, though without certainty, that the reference is to an article of mine in the *Edinburgh Review*, October 1915.

to the principle which they uphold, and which they have all, at some time or other, obscured and checked. I respect those symbols in those who believe in them; they seem to me intolerable only when they are imposed on those who cannot accept them, and when they are considered, in their own form, as an absolute and final form of human thought.

You see then my position, and how I would agree unreservedly with Miss Cavell—a saint of the present war—and, I think, with you too.

I have a special reason for insisting on the religion of the fatherland; it is the one ground on which men of good-will can meet in France. Because of the false humanitarianism which has done us some harm, I do not put the idea of humanity in the first place—and this in order to avoid vagueness, ambiguity and confused opposition. It seems to me better to give a concrete form to our French ideal of humanity by starting from France. It is best to understand one another, and I do not forget humanity. I think it cannot be denied that the war surprised us French on a dangerous slope of moral decline, and it was the danger of France that aroused us. I try to penetrate the significance of this awakening, and to co-ordinate that experience with the very varied experiences of my whole life. Perhaps I was wrong to give my reflections as a kind of answer to some miserable efforts at a politico-religious reaction. I gave them as they presented themselves, and that they might not be lost. For we know not to-day if we shall yet be able to speak to-morrow. Perhaps some day, if I have time, I shall take it up again in the form of thesis and antithesis, endeavouring to interpret the religious and moral evolution of humanity, and the profound sense of that evolution which seems to be the law of life. I have talked of faith because every ideal supposes a faith; because science, with its simple measuring of observable realities, is not in itself a support of moral life, while this moral life is the form without which our human existence would have no more value than that of the humblest animals. I think, in fact, it would be worse, and that humanity would become like an ant-heap at the mercy of the madness of ambition.

I, too, admire Wilson. His manifesto for peace was perfect so far as it went. It was a part of what the people could and should have said. It seemed to me that Wilson finished burying poor Benedict XV. And the terms imposed on Germany are irreproachable. The manifesto for peace was bound to pass above the heads of the belligerents. But the last act, whatever its consequences, seems to me to assure its author a place in the Peace Conference. And that is very important.

THE INFLUENCE OF AUGUSTE COMTE

In his volume *La Religion* there are so many points of analogy between this religion of humanity and that of the Positivist philosopher that more than one must have made the same remark. This is apparent from the subjoined letter to myself, I having been one of those to raise the question. I cannot quote my own words on the subject, as I have no record of them. His answer was as follows:

October 23rd, 1917.

I am not quite able to answer your questions. *I have never read a single work of Comte's.*[1] I had to confess this with shame to a positivist, who delicately reproached me for not having acknowledged in my book what I owed to this great precursor. On the same occasion I pointed out to him a similar omission in regard to some of my conclusions, which border on the philosophy of Bergson, whether published, or as yet unpublished. It is with Bergson—according to his own testimony—that the points of contact are most remarkable.

So far as I can judge, in my ignorance of Comte, there is first the difference that you indicate: Comte denies any spiritual beyond; I am fully disposed to affirm without defining it; I am perfectly conscious of admitting an implicit metaphysic; what I do not admit is the necessity of a learned metaphysic, of a philosophical theology as the foundation of religion and morality. I do not think that such could ever have been its basis, it could only be its completion. As a basis it is always too *rational* in the narrow sense of the word. I have tried to show, right through my book, how a religion of humanity unfolded itself *from the whole religious past of our kind*. It does not seem to me that Comte founded his religion of humanity on the philosophy of religious history. It seems to me that he had an absolute conception—dogmatic and theological, though he did not know it—of humanity. I have said and repeated that humanity does not yet exist, that she is labouring, and that her ideal only defines and will define itself

---

[1] His own italics.

progressively. I am not sure that Comte had as clear and religious an idea of duty as that which I endeavoured to give it in founding it on the notion of social humanity as mother and mistress (*domina et magistra*) of individuals. Precisely because he had an abstract and absolute conception of humanity, Comte endeavoured to create a ready-made cult, which naturally proved impracticable, and which now makes the same impression on our minds as that other improvisation, the revolutionary calendar.

I hold that the religion of humanity is forming and will go on forming itself; that the religions actually existing, but principally the different forms of Christianity, are religions of humanity; that Catholicism is one of them and could have been the best of all; that it is as a result of the failure of Christian religions that those who can no longer live in them have to seek a wider human religion and to promote it alongside Christianity, just as they would have promoted it within Christianity itself if they had remained Christians.

In all this I maintain that I am closer to reality than Comte, with his theory, which is as absolute as scholasticism, of the three states. Thus you will see the difference that there is between the conception of science and its rôle according to Comte, and that in my book; I do not attempt to found religion and the world on positive science, still less on positivist science. I do not say that there is no analogy between my ideas and those of Comte. Certain philosophers of the eighteenth century, the revolutionary cults, as well as Comte himself, mark efforts and steps in the direction of the religion of humanity. I might have indicated their place in my historical synthesis, but I cannot assign my own. I only tried to note, historically, the orientation of human religion. All that is relatively original in my book is that every religion is a religion of humanity, and that religious progress—which is identical with human progress—consists in the realization of a higher and more perfect humanity. Did Comte say this, dear Miss Petre, did he say it? Have others said it as I say it, in accordance with facts? I dare not answer such questions, and I ask them *secundum hominem*, as St Paul would say in my place. Certain analogies between my ideas and those of Comte might be more apparent than real.

WAR OF 1914–1918

Ceffonds, August 26th, 1918.

·   ·   ·   ·   ·

But the war is not ended, although things look better. Like
you, I felt the death of Michel Desjardins. The parents endure
this new trial with great courage.[1] Truly the boy died gloriously.
I often say to myself that these young men realize a life that
is fuller and more fruitful than that of our long years. But the
losses mount terribly, and the contribution of all these young
who have perished would have been more valuable than ours
for the work of the coming peace.

November 17th, 1918.

Behold us at the end of our long trial. The end came more
quickly than one expected and in unforeseen conditions. This
crash of empires is something staggering. Ancient and modern
fall one upon another. Russia is no more; nor Austria;
Germany remains an enigma, but the empire of the Hohen-
zollerns has disappeared. Our peoples survive with the glory
of having been instruments in a great cause. The fraternity of
England and France is, in itself, a considerable historic fact,
from which much may be hoped in the future. The United
States arrived in time, and are bringing us their great President. Humanity has escaped Germanic despotism, and it is
indeed a marvel that it has been saved. But it is not enough
to destroy Babylon, we have now to build Jerusalem.

ON THE LEAGUE OF NATIONS

Paris, January 5th, 1919.

·   ·   ·   ·   ·

I shall read with pleasure your work on the League of Nations.
In my opinion a League of Nations demands, as a necessary
condition, a humanity different from that which actually exists
and a discipline different from that which generally prevails.
It is another humanity that is in the making, that requires
to be made; but at present it is almost wholly waiting to be
made. I have developed this idea in my opening lecture, which
I hope to send you. . . . I have little outside information, but
I think that the best minds are with President Wilson. But
I am not at all sure that our politicians follow or understand

---

[1] The second son died in the war of 1940.

him. Nevertheless, I think that Wilson will realize his principal object, because he knows what he wants and embodies a great power. People will be obliged to yield much to him because of the material power he represents, and this will be so much gained for the moral good that he represents and desires to serve. The League of Nations may thus be organized by people who do not all believe in it, but one may hope that it will still be realized because it is an urgent and a growing need. But it will demand care and devotion and faith.

I admire Wilson very much. He speaks without rhetoric, and announces his programme, which is both realist and ideal, with admirable tact. I have just read his Discourses in Rome; they are magnificent. He alone can dare to say in Rome, to the Italians, that the old Roman word *imperare* must be replaced *naturally* by that of liberty. I hope he has said the same to Benedict XV.

THE RHYTHM OF HUMAN LANGUAGE

Ceffonds, October 3rd, 1923.

All human language is rhythmical and susceptible of musical notation; men sing less melodiously than nightingales, but quite as naturally. I am therefore not surprised that you have been able to divide my prose into rhythm. The contrary would cover me with shame. But I do not think my phrases constitute regular symmetrical strophes, with equal numbers of lines and parallelism. In the preface to a volume that you will soon receive, entitled *La Morale Humaine,* I perceived, with horror, that I had written a sentence two pages long. It was unique, I think, not only in the work itself, but in my whole career as a writer. So I do not think that I write in isometric strophes.

It was in re-reading my translation of the Epistles, which I published last year in my Nouveau Testament, that I found, to my surprise, that my sentences fell into a much more regular cadence than when I write on my own. I was thus led to break up the text of the Epistles into a form suitable for the reader. And in doing this I discovered a symmetrical form of sentence in a large number of passages. I have not myself noticed this in the Gospels, but two Germans, a Bavarian and an Austrian, have remarked it. It is not therefore the simple fact of rhythm that is remarkable in the New Testament, but the existence of a regular studied rhythm in writings that are, for the most part, composed in a vulgar tongue. They are writings declaimed, almost chanted, as would be natural in prophetical and liturgical writings. That is my whole thesis; a very simple one, but I think it carries a considerable significance.

Paris, December 13*th,* 1923.

Dear Miss Petre,

I am glad that my little book[1] pleases you, and I hope that you will be able to place the article of which you speak.

It was not part of my plan to treat of the economic character of moral problems which you mention. I wanted to show that all human problems have a moral aspect—which is essential and too often overlooked. It seems to us also that no human problems are susceptible of a simple, mathematical solution; they are all complex and are capable only of mixed and approximate solutions. There will always be a wide margin to be filled by devotion, sacrifice and sorrow; but we have to reduce the portion of sorrow as far as possible. The problem of the birth-rate is a poignant one for us in France. It is not an economic problem, for it would be easy to provide, socially, for the needs of large families. It is, above all, a moral and national problem. Already, even for the cultivation of our soil, we have to call on the foreigner. Poland is even now sending us a number of agricultural labourers. That is all right, provided they do not lose, by contact with us, their hereditary virtues, and provided they also overcome certain faults of their own. But all this is an insufficient palliative; soon the scarcity of men will be felt everywhere. We are beginning to feel it in higher, and even in elementary, education. What can be the future of a people that is decreasing before one's eyes? In other spheres the economic difficulty may well be the principal one. If these evils are not met in justice by morally advantageous compensation for all, the time will come when the balance will be restored by violence at the expense of the weak. It is by violence that humanity has hitherto escaped, for good or ill, and rather badly than well, from the impasses in which she found herself. When will she seek inspiration in justice and goodness for the regulation of her affairs? The moral solution would always be the best, but how is she to be made to believe this?

It was not possible for me to enter in detail into the good

[1] *La Morale Humaine.*

examples with which animals furnish us.[1] I had to limit myself to saying that, in their world, satisfaction of the sexual instinct was limited by the demands of reproduction. Many birds are monogamous in the breeding season; some birds are so for perpetuity; thus pigeons. I have known a widowed bird fetch, from another dove-cote, the partner needed, but once the couple was formed it was permanent. I did not know the habits of the swan. What you tell me of geese rather surprises me. I often saw, in the farms of Champagne, a gander guarding a band of geese with their young. When, as a little boy, I attended the elementary school at Ambrières, I had a stick to keep off a formidable gander, who walked the street with his family.[2]

Anatole France, as I am told, said that his Abbé Jérôme Coignard would not sign the declaration of the rights of man because it proclaimed too outrageously our superiority over the gorilla. I see that you have something of this philosophy.

We have our elections next spring, and I know not what they will give us. However, it seems probable that the majority of our deputies will be nationalist. May they be such with intelligence and moderation.

Brémond is at Pau, preparing his panegyric of Duchesne. I wish he could be quickly free from these academic rites and entirely occupied with the completion of his great work, of which I desire to read some more volumes.

Ceffonds, June 11th, 1929.

Jean Baruzi tells me that you are at Pontigny, and I suppose you have been there for some time as Paul Desjardins told me, at the beginning of March, that you were coming. You will add a page to the English memories of Pontigny. Would it be indiscreet to ask you whether you are satisfied, that is to say, whether the work in which you are engaged seems to you of increasing utility?

I am also without news of Brémond, to whom I wrote my thanks for the last publications he sent me. His *Rancé*[3] is truly remarkable. . . . And I noted—but do not denounce him—that

---

[1] Reference, of course, to some plea of mine on behalf of the decent lives of many dumb beasts. I had cited some article on the subject of the perversion of animal morals from their domestication by man.

[2] It is clear that his knowledge of geese was more accurate than mine.

[3] *L'Abbé Tempête* (Hachette).

for this volume he did not ask for an *imprimatur*. I think he is plunged in work, and I feel somewhat anxious for his health; but knowing nothing, and not being of the Academy, I dare not say so to him.

I am very busy with my Memoirs, and I may never get through them.[1] If I am alive at the end of this year I will put a final touch to the Memoirs and return to Christian Origins. I am not ill, but am getting older, and find it more and more difficult to live.

Very respectfully and affectionately,

Ceffonds, August 12*th,* 1931.

ON MY ARTICLE ON HIS MEMOIRS

The article has arrived at last and I have read it twice. I thank you for it sincerely. You have marked the various steps of my career very well. The printer puts my birth as February 25th, 1857; I was born February 28th, 34 years, to the day, after Renan.

You would not believe me if I said that I shared your opinion on all points. There are two in particular on which I make some reservations:

P. 664: 'I am sometimes too logical, a French failing'— von Hügel said it before you and I am not sure that he was right. He fed on logic and reasoning much more than I did. In any case, so far as my attitude to the Church is concerned, it was not logic that dominated my steps. If I had followed abstract logical reasoning, I should have left the Church in 1885, or 1893, or, above all, in 1904. I left the Church when it became impossible to survive in it spiritually, and that is why I shall never return to it. In reality, the Roman Church is being transformed into a barracks, with intellectual and moral mobilization. Life can admit of many contradictions, but religious life cannot admit of them in the domain of morality. And the authority of the Church has become profoundly immoral.

You quote Duchesne as a man who understood, etc. I know well what Duchesne understood. I knew Duchesne better than any of his recent panegyrists, von Hügel included. Duchesne did not count on life to resolve the contradictions of which you speak. Duchesne was in the midst of them. We are caught between the necessity and the impossibility of a solution, and

[1] But of course he did.

I fear that we shall not find it. Let us leave Duchesne in peace in his tomb. He was a great savant and rather a great man, but not a man of great faith nor a religious philosopher. It is waste of time to offer him to me as an example.

And you regret, for me the loss of the Church, for the Church the loss of me. It seems to me that the Church cares little for this loss, and she is right, because I was certainly not the man she needed. She would only have done better to say it sooner. As to my own loss, I do not believe in it. My colleague, the Abbé Breuil, who teaches pre-history at the Collège de France, said, not long ago, that our poor race has been on the earth about 50,000 years. The Church is only 2000 years old, and has aged visibly for centuries. I am no prophet, but she has not 50,000 years before her, if the earth remain habitable so long. The world is in labour with a new religion. Look at the East of Europe, a mad people that thinks to give happiness to the world, and behind it the forces of Asia, India, China. What is being prepared there? How will the unification of peoples, towards which we move, be brought about? Do you think the Pope will be its President? No more than the descendants of Caiaphas governed the Roman world. . . . A new era is in the making on the ruins of ancient peoples and ancient religions. Of Christianity there will remain only the spirit, not the framework. And then? Then I am of the religion that is in the making and I am quite willing not to belong to the one that is dying. I am isolated through age and weak health, but I should not be so if I could mingle with those who work according to their lights and their power to the building of the future Jerusalem. My logic is perhaps not so absolute nor so narrow as you think.

Everyone, in this poor world, does as best he can. . . .

We are all individuals, and each one of us presents a personal case.

ON THE DEATH OF BRÉMOND

Ceffonds, August 18th, 1933.

Dear Miss Petre,

I have just learned of the death of our friend Brémond. I expected it, but I am none the less appalled by this great loss. I shall miss him greatly during my remaining days. Knowing no one of his family, I can only address myself to you, to say how deeply I share a sorrow that is not exclusively that of his family, etc.

On his Volume 'Georges Tyrrell et Henri Brémond', 1936

Ceffonds, August 19th, 1936.

Having, against my will, some days of leisure . . . I have begun to classify my correspondence, and have made a beginning with the letters of Brémond, an important collection, of which the reading has profoundly moved me. What I felt was that, as the silence of his heirs at least demonstrated their inability to serve his memory and as I had no reason to suspect their good will, it would be well to write some simple pages about him, exposing and recalling the true character of his relations with Tyrrell, examining Tyrrell's true religious position, and showing how the religious thought of Brémond, which should have received its final expression in the volume on the supposed quietism of Fénelon, has been little understood although his works in general more or less disclose it. The recent Academical pronouncements around his empty chair have been of a distressing mediocrity. One would say that these gentlemen understood nothing, and that they continue to refer to Bossuet on the question of 'pur amour',[1] just as they refer to him on his treatment of the Biblical question against Richard Simon, and on the legend of the Saints of Provence. It makes one despair of the human intellect.

I do not conceal from myself that the work in question would be particularly delicate, for it seems to me that Brémond's thought and mine on the profound significance of mysticism were not far apart, and this will scandalize some. I do not want to cause the least annoyance to his brothers. Although it seems, at first sight, most improbable that Brémond did not leave at least a sketch of his volume on the Fénelon-Bossuet controversy, it is not really impossible that this volume was so easy to write that he reserved its composition for the last and that death surprised him. Have the kindness to tell me what you know and what you think about this.

I suspect that Brémond, like the late Duchesne, of good and spiritual memory, kept nothing of his correspondence, so that they will have found among his papers little or nothing concerning me. I think I wrote him a letter on the first news of his illness; it has not been returned to me. Whether it has been kept or suppressed is of little importance. Given the

[1] The mystical question which was a special point in Brémond's work.

vicissitudes of his career I doubt if Brémond had any wish
to preserve letters written to him.

I do not know whether I shall be able to realize my plan . . .
but you will understand why I ask for your views and your
advice.

.   .   .   .   .   .

Ceffonds, August 30th, 1936.

I have no wish to scandalize anyone in heaven or on earth,
but I have a right to refute the Academic lies that suffocated
me in the recent discourses at the reception of Brémond's
successor. What I have to say should scandalize no one. But
Brémond certainly does not belong to the botanical species
of *Catholicus Vulgaris* (into which they have also tried to meta-
morphize Duchesne).

Ceffonds, September 2nd, 1936.

I positively do not see that my book on Tyrrell and Brémond
could scandalize anyone. I utilize documents published by
yourself, and, so far as Brémond is personally concerned, I turn
to the Academy for the foolish things that were spoken *against*
him on the occasion of the solemn reception of his successor.

.   .   .   .   .   .

On my Book 'My Way of Faith'

Ceffonds, January 16th, 1937.

I have received your book and am glad it has appeared during
my life-time. Not that I wish to refute it, quite the contrary.
I have already learned a good deal, though I have not finished
it. Naturally, I first turned to the section concerning von
Hügel, Brémond and Tyrrell. Your judgment on von Hügel
seems to me definitive; I should add, for his last years, a somewhat morbid fixed idea, a consequence also of his tempera-
ment. As to Brémond, you tell us a good deal, especially about
the crisis through which he passed before leaving the Society
of Jesus. . . . What impresses me most is the perfect sincerity
of your literary approach. That is, perhaps, what will dis-
concert your orthodox readers; I personally am edified by it;
I am rather surprised to find that, during these last years,
I held a larger place than you in Brémond's life. . . .

Ceffonds, January 19*th,* 1937.

I have at last finished my first, somewhat rapid, reading of the fine book. I am very pleased. . . .

One must turn to you to know the truth about the religious crisis of Brémond, and to me to know the religious philosophy that Brémond was elaborating behind his great work. . . .

Ceffonds, November 16*th,* 1938.

It is well to inform you of what is passing here. Feeling that my strength is declining more and more, I have begun to settle my affairs. On October 31st a big van came from Paris to take all my religious books—fifty cases—to be deposited in the library of the University of Paris. . . .

I have now to classify my papers . . . to destroy a fair amount, especially the letters of persons still living, who might be compromised if they fell under hostile eyes. I have kept all your letters. If you want them back . . . my literary executor would return them to you. For my own part, I would like to combine them, as documents, with the von Hügel correspondence.[1]

PAUL DESJARDINS AND PONTIGNY

Ceffonds, July 4*th,* 1939.

I should have liked to write sooner to tell you how I feel for Paul Desjardins in his sorrow.[2] I have the happiest memory of M. Raverat, whom I met several times at Pontigny. I did not foresee that the 'Union pour la Vérité' was about to disappear. I have sometimes criticized it, but I always wished it well. And now, before the coming events, I feel, above all, my helplessness. . . .

PAPERS

Ceffonds, September 20*th,* 1939.

My life could not fail to be upset by events. Nothing grave as yet, but my strength diminishes. I walk with ever greater difficulty, and the least effort, even intellectual, tires me. I ask myself, given the difficulty of communications, what will happen to my papers if I depart before the end of the torment, and if there be no one to ensure their preservation. . . .

[1] I left him free—M.D.P.
[2] The death of his friend Raverat.

Ceffonds, Easter Sunday, 1940.

It was through you that I learnt of the death of Paul Desjardins. I hastened to send my sincere condolence to his
widow....For some time I have lived in a kind of whirlwind,
disturbed in my habits, growing ever weaker, to the point of
not being able to complete the classification of my papers....
The world needs great leaders....Never have I realized so
clearly how little a weak man, whose pen is his only weapon,
can do.[1]

[1] He died June 1st.

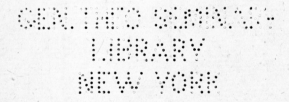

CAMBRIDGE: PRINTED BY W. LEWIS, M.A., AT THE UNIVERSITY PRESS